W9-DIO-067

EX LIBRIS

# THEATER
## A CRASH COURSE

# THEATER
# A CRASH COURSE

ROB GRAHAM

WATSON-GUPTILL PUBLICATIONS
*New York*

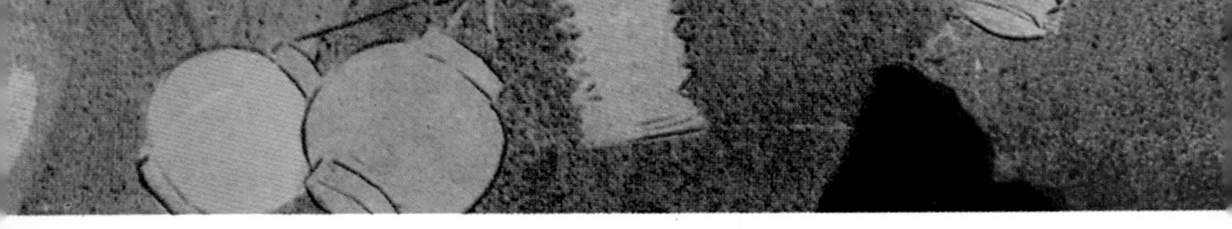



First published in the United States in 1999
by Watson-Guptill Publications, a division of
BPI Communications, Inc., 1515 Broadway,
New York, NY 10036



Library of Congress Catalog Card Number: 99-61087

ISBN 0-8230-0981-5

*This book was conceived, designed,
and produced by*
THE IVY PRESS LIMITED
2/3 St Andrews Place
Lewes, East Sussex, BN7 1UP

*Art Director:* PETER BRIDGEWATER
*Editorial Director:* SOPHIE COLLINS
*Designer:* JANE LANAWAY
*Project Editor:* HELEN CLEARY
*Editor:* GRAPEVINE PUBLISHING SERVICES
*DTP Designer:* CHRIS LANAWAY
*Illustrations:* MADELEINE HARDIE
*Picture Researcher:* VANESSA FLETCHER

Reproduction and printing in Hong Kong by
Hong Kong Graphic and Printing Ltd.

1 2 3 4 5 6 7 8 9 10/08 07 06 05 04 03 02 01 00 99

This book is typeset in Bauer Bodoni 8/11.

DEDICATION

To Joe and Erin

# Contents

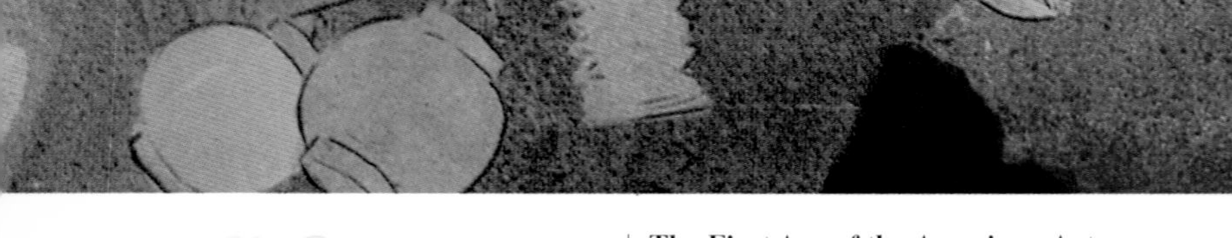

**Behind the Scenes**
Theater design, sets, staging, lighting, acting techniques, and philosophies. The technical information that will enlighten you as to how it all takes shape, and ways in which it can go wrong.

# Introduction

*This book is intended to help you know a bit more about one of the most wonderful activities human beings have ever dreamed up—live theater. You probably already know quite a lot about its essence, even if you've never studied it. After all, putting on funny hats and pretending to be someone else is an integral part of most people's childhood (and no matter what any actor or director may loftily claim, theater still operates partly at that level. As Laurence Olivier once said, "it's no fit job for a grown man"!) Besides, acting is the greatest "spectator sport" in the world, greater even than football!*

Laurence Olivier as Archie Rice (1957), a trademark role.

*Theater has been with the human race virtually since it stood upright (I know, I know, there are still plenty of knuckles dragging on the floor). Although in the 20th century it has had to move from center stage to make room for radio,*

"This isn't what I trained for!" Actor pretending to be a mushroom.

*movies, and television, it hasn't gone into the wings to sulk. If anything, it just rushed off for yet another costume change. After modernism, theater has found new ways of telling those stories we love to hear. Ways that try to celebrate all over again the wonder and magic of the "live" performance unattainable by celluloid or videotape. Also, in the West it still provides the training ground for many actors, directors, and writers, while in the emerging Third World it has yet again proved its superiority as an accessible means of voicing the pain, anger, and sometimes joy, of the growing numbers of dispossessed.*

**Timeline**
More of a contextual chronology than a timeline, because writers, directors, and movements are constantly overlapping. A highly idiosyncratic list of major and less major events happening at the time the protagonists were living, to illuminate the world they inhabited and the zeitgeist of the period.

"Darling, you're standing on my frock." Sir Noel and Gertie Lawrence.

*Its history and diversity is unbelievable. From tribal rituals to avant-garde performances; from religious festivals to well-made plays; from one-person shows to*

**PROMPT BOX**
A useful little gem you can use to impress your theatrical friends: gossip, bitchiness, or the extracurricular activities of some of the major names.

It's a miracle! Audiences loved these amateur religious shows.

*casts of thousands; from short sketches to serious tests of bladder control; from light amusements to profound philosophy; from mild satire to something worth dying for; theater has said and shown it all. There are two ways of making sense of life—religion and dramatic reenactment, and sometimes even these get confused with each other. The clerical robes of office and the costume of the actor are not that far apart; and both can and do require the wearing of funny hats.*

*This book is necessarily selective in its attempt to convey the vastness of world theater, and is sometimes opinionated and irreverent, but then, so is theater.*

John Gielgud's classic *Hamlet* in 1933. Love the necklace, sweetie!

**How This Course Works**

Each double-page spread is devoted to a theatrical movement or a group of playwrights, actors, or directors with something in common, and the story proceeds more or less chronologically. On each spread there are some regular features. It won't take you long to figure them out but check the boxes on pages 8-11 for more information.

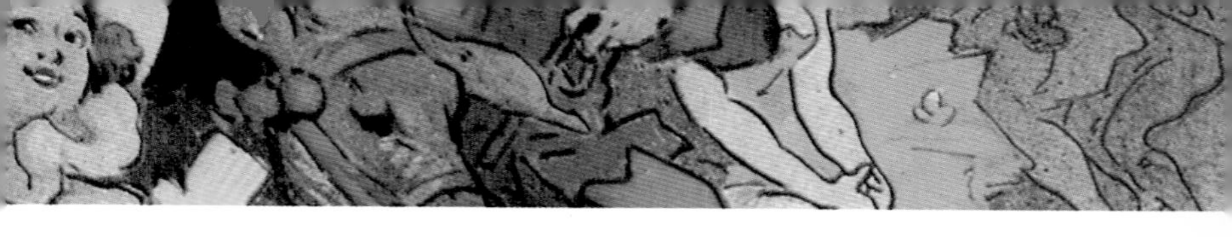

Actors like playing the Fool—not too many lines and they get all the laughs.

*More than any other art form you care to mention, theater is a dangerous business.*

*It is to governments and monarchies what Lear's fool was to Lear—an amusing idiot who often speaks the deepest of truths, no matter how painful or dangerous, and it is no accident that dictators take it very seriously. On the other hand, it is also used as a vehicle to promote the silliest and most pretentious notions imaginable, and has often been a refuge for certifiable lunatics. This book tries to convey the head, heart, guts, soul, and toenail clippings that make up theater.*

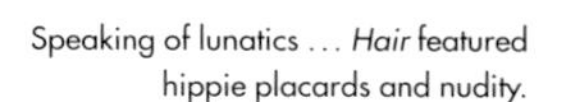

ROB GRAHAM

### Supporting Roles

*Other performers worthy of note alongside the major names (and often producing much more interesting work).*

Speaking of lunatics ... *Hair* featured hippie placards and nudity.

**38,000–5000 B.C.** Cave paintings in Asia, Africa, and Europe represent men and women dancing, probably one of the oldest forms of expression.

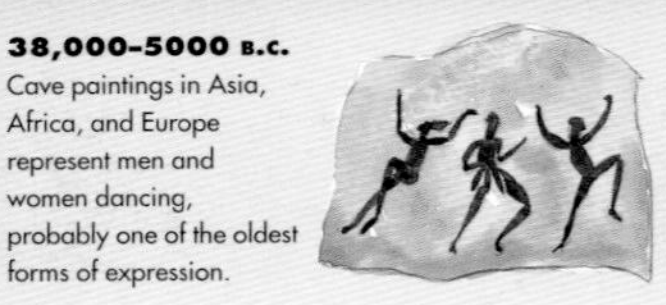

**25,000 B.C.** Early Stone Age hunters start carving antler, bone, and ivory, incising everyday implements, and making little figurines.

**c.7500 B.C.** The domestic dog will become a hunting companion, a protector, an object of affection or loathing, and a friend to humans, and more than 400 breeds will be developed.

4000 B.C.

# "That's the Last Time I Play Mammoth!"

## Prehistory, Cave Paintings, Ritual, and Dance

*Before the Greeks and Romans, about whom we know relatively little, before the Egyptians, about whom we know even less, before, in fact, all that we refer to as "ancient" theater, how did folks enjoy a night on the town?*

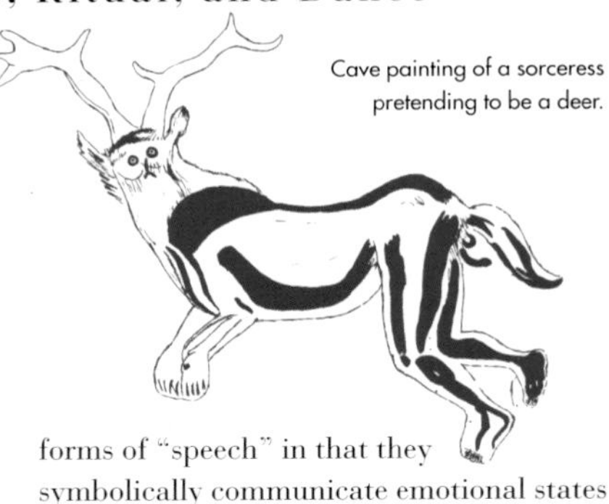

Cave painting of a sorceress pretending to be a deer.

In his *Poetics*, ARISTOTLE (384–322 B.C.) mentions ("Drones on a Lot About" would be nearer the mark) "imitation" and how instinctive it is to the human race. Perhaps he was putting the case too strongly; it is probably more an aptitude than an instinct, but a powerful aptitude for all that. And this aptitude for imitation has been with us for a long time. We don't know who the first person was to find it fun to jump around in a mask or animal skin (nor do we know what his friends thought of him), but dance and the use of masks/costume must have developed alongside the earliest rituals. Both are forms of "speech" in that they symbolically communicate emotional states too deep for words (or grunts).

Cave paintings in southern France clearly show men dressed "as deer," as part of some hunting ritual (or a fashion statement?). Animal impersonation may well have been the earliest form of acting ("Mammoth in Boots"?).

**PROMPT BOX**

"Flyting" is the exchange of insults in a stylized manner. The Greeks used it, as did Shakespeare and many modern writers. It has also formed the banter of much double-act comedy. Sometimes it is good-natured, other times not so. For example, barristers engage in a fair bit of nasty flyting, while politicians do little else.

**6000 B.C.** The island of Crete is occupied. The Minoan (called after the legendary King Minos) Bronze Age culture will reach a peak in about 1600 B.C., when it is destroyed by the Myceneans.

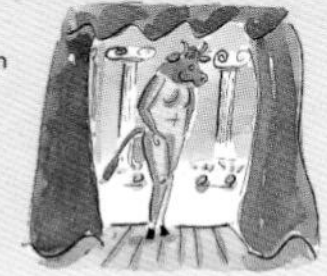

**4400 B.C.** The Halafians in Northern Syria construct circular domed buildings.

**4000 B.C.** The world's population reaches roughly 85 million.

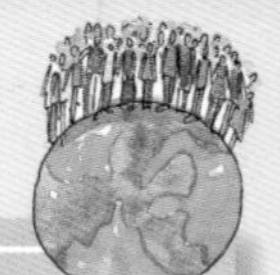

The principal theories influencing our notions of ritual were formed by a group of wild things called the "Cambridge school" at the turn of the 20th century, and most notably by James Frazer in *The Golden Bough* (1890) and Jane Harrison in *Themis* (1912). These scholars, supported by studies in the history of religion, archaeology, anthropology, etc., argued that early rituals were enacted to ensure social well-being. Although they probably didn't get out enough, they had a point. Ritual has always been one of the keystones of theater history. Like theater, ritual emphasizes the doing of things—the concrete and the actual rather than the merely metaphysical. However, unlike theater, which merely says a few things about social relationships, ritual reinforces or changes them.

## Supporting Roles

*One ritual concerned the selection of the divine "god-king-hero" to rule a community for one year. Then he was killed by a successor—who consequently inherited his sterling qualities and also ruled for a year until he was killed, and so on. (Could there have been a play entitled* The Man Who Certainly Does Not Want to Be King, but Would Be Happy to Serve on the Selection Committee?).

Bronze cult wagon from the seventh century B.C. showing more strange deer rituals.

The central preoccupations of early rituals seem to have been maintaining order, sex, planting/harvesting crops, sex, new year celebrations, sex, the installation of a king, and generally controlling the universe. Oh, and sex.

Many took a common narrative, e.g., the god-king-hero fights an opposing power (bad weather or natural disasters, high infant mortality, neighboring tribe, etc.); he suffers badly—sometimes he even dies; he is resurrected; and thus the myth of creation is symbolically recreated; there is a sacred marriage, a triumphal procession, and finally a settling of destinies for all the characters concerned. If only life were that simple.

"Is he a friend of yours, dear?" Cave painting of hunter dressed as his prey, 15,000–10,000 B.C.

**3300 B.C.** Thin, flat stones used in Egypt for grinding up malachite (used in eye painting) develop into significant works of art.

**3000 B.C.** Palaces at Knossos and Phaestos in Crete, the earliest known examples of European architecture, are built, possibly by settlers from Egypt.

**c. 2600–2500 B.C.** Funerary objects including effigies, armor, and personal possessions are placed in the royal tombs of Ur.

4000~500 B.C.

# A Horus Line

## Passion in the Pyramids

Set for a pyramid play.

*Egypt had "pyramid" plays, coronation festival plays, "heb seds" (coronation jubilees), and passion plays dating back to almost 4000 B.C. There were also Ra (sun god) plays about his nocturnal fight with Apophis, snake god of the underworld; Ra always won.*

The most famous passion play was the *Osiris Passion Play*, performed at Abydos between 1887 and 1849 B.C. As always, this concerned the murder and dismemberment of Osiris, an early king (who subsequently became a god), by his brother Seth, and the reassembling of his body by his wife-sister (yes, that's what it says) Isis and their son, Horus. Of course you can guess which part they always had the most trouble finding.

The performance included battles on land and water, voyages on the Nile, and a scary resurrection scene. The action took several days to complete and audiences joined in the fighting, half supporting bad Seth, and half yelling for Horus. The actor/soldiers who slew Osiris were possibly sacrificed (thereby setting the tone for the future treatment of "extras").

The pyramid plays were religious ceremonies with "acted" sections about either the ascent of a deceased king's soul

**PROMPT BOX**

The first actor ever mentioned in recorded history was one I-kher-nefert (hence the ancient preperformance chant of actors: "I-kher-nefert remember my lines!"). He was also the first real actor: his account of producing a dramatic celebration of Osiris at Abydos extols his great performance as Horus, his building a boat for Osiris, the "splendid costume" with which he bedecked an actor, ad nauseum.

**c. 1800 B.C.** A taboo against eating pork appears among some peoples of the Near East; they are sheepherding peoples and the pig is a domesticated animal of their farming enemies.

**1567–1320 B.C.** The first glassware is made; molded glass is decorated with colored trails, solid glass engraved, and colored rods fused to make mosaic glass.

**1122 B.C.** During the Chou dynasty, sacred rituals of worship begin to incorporate a dramatic element.

## Supporting Roles

*As he "killed" the demon Apophis, a priest would chant: "I have cut his vertebrae at the neck . . . I have made him nonexistent; his name is not; his children are not; he is not and his family is not; his false-door is not: his heirs are not. His egg shall not last, nor shall his seed be knit together." Now that is what I call Final.*

to become one of the Imperishable Stars, or the King's resurrection (or, if he was seriously popular, both). The main characters were, once again, Osiris and Horus. Osiris would have represented the dead king and Horus the living one (this role was sometimes played by the new king himself).

The resurrection of the dead king was the centerpiece of the whole action and would have called for a physical presence to rise from the grave. When a priest intoned to the corpse of Osiris, "Your Highness! Cast off the bricks—the sand—the wrappings that bind you!" it was a situation *screaming out* for a "body" to rise up spookily. Only a senior priest could have that role (and, no doubt, the most outrageous costume wardrobe could find).

The coronation plays celebrated the accession to power of a new pharaoh, and each separate "scene" was acted out at various points along the route of a procession. A papyrus manuscript of one example of this kind of drama was found in a worm-eaten state by the pharaoh Shabaka around 800 B.C. He had it carefully copied onto a stone slab for his father. This stone still exists, though it has proved difficult to read, since in more modern times subsequent generations of Egyptians drilled a hole in it and used it as a millstone (which is just what the West did with Shakespeare's scripts!).

**Behind the Scenes**
There was some sort of stage machinery evident in these texts—usually in the form of boats and carriages to carry Osiris and Horus. Elaborate masks, both for the deities and other, animal, figures were made. Their supporting shoulder straps can be seen in contemporary hieroglyphics.

Horus being a hero. Before the advent of Animatronics, real hippos were used.

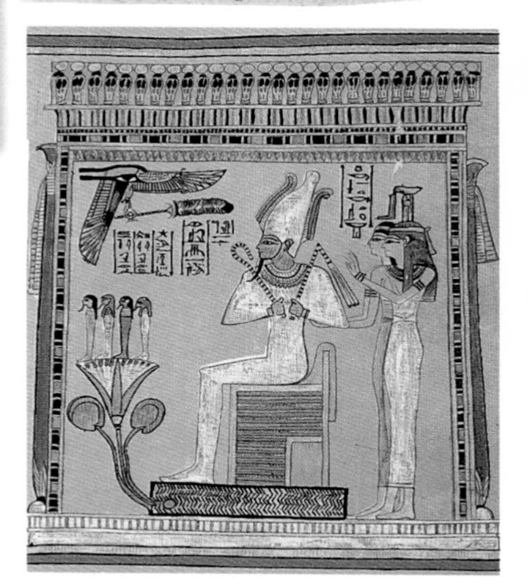

"You've overdone the green again, girls." Osiris gets his makeup done in the trailer by the goddesses Isis and Nephthys. From the *Book of the Dead*.

**1000-500 B.C.** Mycenaean pottery is painted in geometric patterns, in particular the "key" pattern.

**600 B.C.** The Roman forum ceases to be used as a cemetery.

**570 B.C.** The Greek philosopher Anaximander, considered to be the founder of astronomy, is also credited with producing the first map.

1200~500 B.C.

# Tragedy, Comedy, and Hemorrhoids

## The Famous Greeks

*Although there is evidence of Greek drama in Syria from about 1200 B.C., most of what we think of as classical Greek theater was produced in the 5th century B.C. Their word* theatron *("watching space") gave us the name "theater." The earliest dramas took place at the five- or six-day festivals in honor of the god Dionysus (seems like a good idea). The first theater buildings were wooden, but later semicircular ones were built of stone utilizing natural hollows in hillsides.*

### Three Unities

Aristotle, though not a dramatist, laid down the basic do's and don'ts of classical tragedy in his *Poetics* (around 330 B.C.). In particular, all drama was to observe the Three Unities (not a Motown girl group) of time, place, and action, although he goes on to explain only what the unity of Action was, not the other two. Nevertheless, this stuff influenced the theater's development until at least the 17th century.

The most notable ruins are at Epidaurus, Thoricus, and the Theater of Dionysus at Athens, where the works of *Aeschylus* (?525–456 B.C.), *Sophocles* (?496–406 B.C.), and *Euripides* (?480–406 B.C.) were performed. They seated around 14,000 people—about half the population of Athens—and, while some accounts say women weren't allowed in, others suggest the heady mix of tragedies, comedies, satyr plays, flowing wine, and all those phalluses was so overwhelming that men fainted and women had miscarriages. The plays were also very long, and, although there is no record of hemorrhoids, we all know what sitting on a stone seat for long periods can do.

Basically, classical Greek drama fell into three forms: tragedy, satyr, and comedy. Tragedy wrestled with the big political

**PROMPT BOX**

The existing Theater of Dionysus, mentioned above, is actually of Roman build (to Greek design with Roman additions up to A.D. 61). There are only five pieces of rock on the site which are confirmed to be from 5th-century Greece.

**534 B.C.** Pisistratus, tyrant of Athens, introduces a contest in Tragedy as part of the festival of "The Great Dionysia."

**524 B.C.** Siddhartha Gautama abandons asceticism; sitting under the famous Bo tree at Benares, he has a vision of what he must teach. In time he will become the Buddha.

**300 B.C.** Roman hairdressers are familiar with the art of hair tinting and can bleach hair with Savon de Hesse.

**Protruding Appendages**

Piety apart, since the whole affair was in honor of Dionysus, the god of wine and boinking, all texts were basically about sex. Note, the word tragedy comes from *tragos* (goat) and *ode* (song)—satyrs were naked half animals who did indecent things to women (and each other), and most characters wore phalluses.

issues (life, death, the gods, will-the-sky-fall-on-our-heads?), the satyr (half man, half animal—usually goat) poked fun at them, while the comedy laughed at everyday life. The first known producer/director was Thespis (hence "thespian"), who, it is said, "invented" the actor around 550 B.C. when in one of his "productions" he had someone step forward and answer the chorus—thus creating stage dialogue. The next great writers were Aeschylus, Sophocles, and Euripides, who wrote tragedies and satyr plays, and Aristophanes (?448–?380 B.C.) and Menander (?160–?120 B.C.), who wrote comedies. The Dionysian festival plays took the form of a competition between local poets who would present three tragedies and a satyr play which dealt with a single myth or subject. This play grouping was known as a tetralogy, and the *Oresteia*, written by Aeschylus in 458 B.C., is one of the best examples. Sophocles' *Oedipus Tyrannus* (c. 430 B.C.), although not as widely known, features one of the most famous, if least understood, characters in theater (and later, psychoanalytic) history—that geezer who loved his mother.

A couple of thespians staggering along the morning after their opening-night party.

**Behind the Scenes**

The Greek theater developed the orchestra ("dancing space"): a level, circular, earth-floored area in front of the rectangular stage which had dressing areas on each side. The stage roof was used for acting, too—probably for the entrance of any gods (i.e., *deus ex machina*—"god out of the machine"). There was also a crane (*mechane*) for "flying" actors and a platform on wheels (*ekkyklema*) for showing gory tableaux scenes.

Sometimes the mixture of searing heat, stone seats, violent deaths, and Dionysian excess was too much for some of the participants.

**283 B.C.** The great Alexandrian lighthouse—one of the Seven Wonders of the World—is built on Pharos.

**63 B.C.** Mithridates VI of Pontus, having used poison homeopathically as an antidote against assassination, has to be helped to commit suicide by a Gaulish servant.

**364 B.C.** The first known raised stage is erected in Rome; the first permanent stone theater will be built in 55 B.C.

250 B.C.~A.D. 500

# "Never Work with Animals..."

## Rome and Pantomime

*Whatever you've heard about the Romans, it was probably all true. Yes, they had a theater, but it was entirely lifted from the Greeks, and anyway it came a poor second to breakneck chariot races, gladiatorial fights to the death, and hunting Christians with pack animals. And why not? Rome had its dramatic festivals from the 6th century B.C. called* ludi *(meaning "games"), but the biggest attractions tended to be rope dancing and boxing rather than more cultural pursuits.*

**Simply Beastly**

At the turn of the millennium, tigers, crocodiles, giraffes, bison, and rhinoceroses were imported to fight each other (or Christians). In A.D. 80 the Colosseum staged "games" lasting one hundred days, during which nine thousand animals were slaughtered. One time, bears hidden in a theatrical "setting" of woodland and hills killed a criminal dressed as Orpheus. Where was his social worker? In the artists' bar, perhaps.

"Do you know, Tarquin, I've got a funny feeling these aren't men in animal suits after all!"

Translations of Greek farces crept into these events around 240 B.C., but not a single play survives with a plot invented by a Roman. They were far more interested in the cut and thrust (literally) of show business than all that intellectual stuff. The local magistrate who organized the games would book an actor-manager (Roman invention), who had his own troupe of slaves and foreigners as performers, to create a good show. If the play was popular, the actor-manager received money or some special gift, and if it wasn't, they featured on the top of the bill—with the lions. This system inevitably produced claques of hired applauders who would manipulate audience response by cheering favored productions and booing others (thus giving some idiot the idea of inventing an entirely redundant career suitable only for oleaginous ne'er-do-wells: that of Critic).

There was no satirical comedy, for, unlike the Greeks, the Roman court was intolerant of self-mockery. Tragedy followed, based on Greek models, but comprising more blood and guts rhetoric

**A.D. 1–500** Roman artists paint murals portraying everyday life, landscapes, and genre scenes.

**472** Vesuvius erupts; falls of ash are reported as far away as Constantinople.

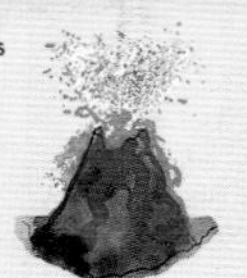

**527** The monk Dionysus Exiguus introduces the chronological notation Anno Domini, A.D.

A typical matinée performance in the Colosseum, around A.D. 100.

of the dull-but-earnest "For King and Country" sort than any kind of philosophical debate.

The dramatic form for which Rome is most remembered is comedy and the pantomimes. The most admired exponents of the former were PLAUTUS (?254–?184 B.C.) and TERENCE (?190–159 B.C.) (who also wrote tragedies). Both men relied entirely on Greek plots, which they Romanized and supplemented with lots of bawdy jokes and vulgarities (Plautus) or a few high-minded titters (Terence). However, it has to be said, the five-act format for tragedy created by writers like Terence and SENECA (?4 B.C.–A.D. 65) became the standard for Shakespeare.

The pantomime, which saw off tragedy, was a very popular grotesque dumb show performed by a masked dancer/clown accompanied by a sort of sung chorus. It is arguable there is something perpetually essential to theater here; a robust visual, spatial, and physical art form in no way subservient to literature (a mere aspect of theater, after all). The snooty Roman upper classes despised the pantomimes, but fortunately their opinions were generally disregarded. One aristocrat who loved it so much that he often performed himself was the emperor Nero. Enough said?

**Nymphs and Shepherds**

Another form favored by both Roman and Greek courts was the pastoral drama. These were essentially lyrical poems that idealized the joys of a rural lifestyle over the corrupt urban one. To say they were rather fanciful would be churlish. After all, what's wrong with stories about nymphs and shepherds frolicking in the fields while singing about nature, duty, honor, and unrequited love? Nothing at all, as far as I'm concerned.

**Behind the Scenes**

The Romans and the Greeks between them gave us a clear distinction between actor and audience, the control of audience by entrance fee and selection, dressing rooms, and foyers. The Romans added a proper proscenium area and curtain, behind which was a permanent acting/location space. Seating was covered and the whole tiered, oval *antifeatro*, holding 20,000, provided a spectacle with more actors, machines, and extras than ever before or since. Like the man said, nothing succeeds like excess.

**970** Hrosvitha of Gandersheim, a German nun, writes six plays based on Terence's comedies, which will be acted by her sister nuns.

**c.1000–1010** In France, the *Chanson de Roland*, an epic poem, celebrates Charlemagne and his court and the legends that had grown up around them.

**1017–1050** Bernay Abbey is built, the earliest surviving Norman church.

950~1550

# Here Comes the Passion Wagon

## "It's All a Mystery to Me..."

*Around A.D. 470 , as Rome declined, the Roman church came down on theater like a ton of bricks, despising the preference people showed for comedy to worship. Undoubtedly some sort of drama must have taken place, for the human spirit has always been stronger than any church. Most likely it was linked to secular festivals in winter or spring, although there are no records of dramatic activity until the liturgical texts of the 10th century (and even these would probably have been a part of the church services).*

**Behind the Scenes**

Both on the wagons and the fixed stages, Hell, with its gaping mouth and belching smoke, would be on the right and Heaven on the left. The central character(s) such as Adam and Eve would be hauled between the two (sounds like normal married life). The action would not be confined to the wagons, either. Characters (e.g., Herod) might "rage" all over the street if the passion took them.

Beginning with the *Quem Queritis trope* (Latin questions and answers between priest and congregation), services expanded to include a bit of acting-out from the Bible (the Slaughter of the Innocents was a good one). Eventually the Mystery and Morality plays developed outside the church (thrown out actually by Pope Innocent in 1210, fount of human kindness that he was).

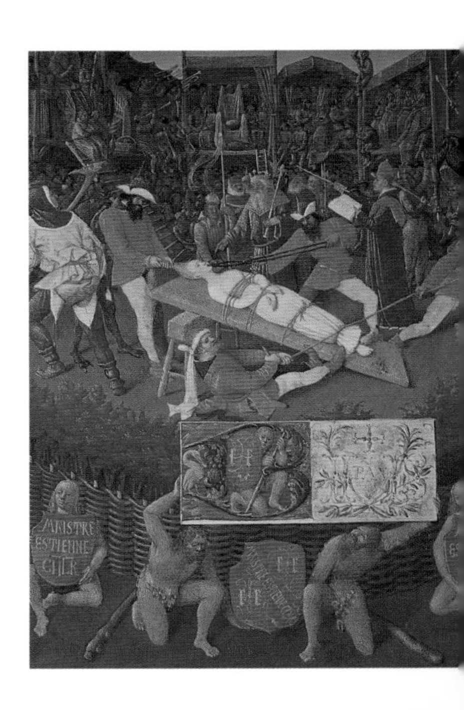


*The Martyrdom of St. Apollonia*, one of the Miracle plays (painted by J. Fouquet). "No, you can't call your agent. Just keep still."

**1230** An English chaplain writes a book of devotional advice for three sisters; *The Ancrene Riwle* is considered the greatest prose work of the Early Middle English period.

**1373** The Dutch develop an early form of the canal lock.

**1533** Ivan IV comes to power; under his rule, Russia will become a centrally administered state. He will be called Ivan the Terrible because of his reign of terror against the hereditary nobility.

During the 12th century, nonliturgical, vernacular plays based on biblical stories were performed at festivals, such as Christmas. These were called the Mystery Cycles (the "mystery" was redemption—nothing to do with wheeled transportation appearing before its time). Local lads from the crafts guilds and companies performed these "passions" on rough wagons in procession through the streets or on fixed, circular stages. They lasted several days, and, being a festival, a fair bit of drinking went on (thereby starting another thespian tradition). This theater was probably very robust and pleasurable for all concerned, a true communal celebration of God, civic pride, and creativity in the acting and making of props and costumes. And not a word of Latin was heard. This no doubt added to the undoing of such theater, since it was primarily the church, ever the killjoy, which silenced these amateur players late in the 16th century.

A Miracle play which appears to show the Devil getting dental treatment in a box theater.

## Supporting Roles

*The Devil was a favorite character, both comic and frightening. His entrance was accompanied with much banging of pots and kettles, and he often somewhat dangerously deployed fireworks. A stage direction from* The Castle *runs: "He that shall play Baal look that he have gunpowder… in pipes in his hands, in his ears, and in his arse when he go to battle."*

The Moralities (known as "Interludes" in their day) came later, with the best known, *The Castle of Perseverance* and *Everyman*, written in the early 15th century. Moralities, though varied, had a common concern in presenting the struggle between good and evil for the soul of man. *The Castle* covered the history of mankind from birth to death. It contained the seven deadly sins, the seven virtues, and the three enemies of mankind—the World, the Flesh, and the Devil. *Everyman* focuses on the final moments of man when he realizes what he needs to do to gain salvation (a great deal in most cases). Above all, having a laugh was not on the agenda.

**1040** Macbeth murders Duncan I of Scotland and claims the kingdom; he will rule until 1057, when he is killed in battle by Duncan's son, Malcolm.

**1080** Constantine the African, a physician who has studied medicine and magic at Babylon, translates Arabian, Jewish, and Greco-Roman medical treatises into Latin.

**1133** St. Bartholomew's Fair is founded in Smithfield, London; for 700 years it will be a venue for music, dancing, and plays.

950~1550

# Pig's Blood, Guts, and Explosions

## European Mysteries

*Though Mysteries on the Continent developed much as did those in England, there were differences. The French were more spectacular than anyone in their sets and effects, the Spanish went in for realistic torture scenes, the Italians sang very nicely, and the Germans had their wagons in the town square long before anyone else was even out of bed. Mostly the stories were the same, with national preferences. It was the development of a wonderful sense of theatricality that separates these plays from the English ones.*

A Mystery play showing devils besieging a king. Note the proximity to the church and also to the "Mouth of Hell."

The most well-known French text was the anonymous *Play of Adam* (*Le Jeu d'Adam*) from the 12th century. It was a dramatized sermon, but it was notable for some very ambitious effects and varied types of characterization.

Basically it dealt with the creation and fall of Adam and Eve, the Cain and Abel story, and a few bits and pieces from the Old Testament. At its end Adam and Eve are tied in chains by four men dressed as devils, and hauled across the stage to a smoke-belching Hell (I know people who'd pay for that). Another manuscript, of the plays performed at Valenciennes in the 16th century, describes in detail how machinery turned a "golden ray" behind the head of God, and how the Mouth of Hell spouted fire and smoke before Lucifer rose wondrously in the air on a fiery dragon. Planned explosions, e.g., blowing up false idols "as if of their own accord," were common too. The French

**Behind the Scenes**
Pageantry, a secular entertainment usually about the shenanigans of kings, developed at the same time as the Mysteries. Pageants involved huge processional wheeled floats of ships and castles (propelled by rows of heaving men inside), which were big enough to allow crowds of "soldiers" to assault their decks and battlements by climbing ladders.

**1307** An ordinance prohibits barber-surgeons in London from displaying blood in their shop windows for the purposes of advertisement.

**1403** To prevent the spread of infectious diseases, Venice requires all travelers from the Levant to be isolated in a detention hospital for 40 days (*quaranta giorni* = quarantine).

**1533** German mathematician Gemma Frisius devises a new method of surveying to replace the laborious method of pacing out distances.

The Winter Solstice, one of several traditional festivities and an important time for medieval folk to have a carnival.

also went in for endurance. A cycle at Bourges in 1536 took 40 days to complete (and 40 nights of scene changing). Some of the plays started at dawn and were 12 hours long with barely an intermission (don't you just wish you'd been there?).

## Supporting Roles

*Ever heard of an actor "dying on stage"? Well, sometimes ... At Valenciennes, the Devil had to remove Judas's soul via his stomach (and you thought* Alien *was original!), which exploded, spilling out his guts (more blood in bladders). This was after Judas had been "hanged" (how much would Jack Nicholson expect for this?). On occasion it really was curtains for the poor schlemiel (see page 141). It's a dangerous business, this acting stuff.*

In one of the Spanish Mysteries there is a stage direction to cut off a saint's breasts "with the greatest possible cruelty": to achieve the effect in one performance at Metz in 1468 an actor wore cardboard breasts filled with animal blood. (Pig's blood in a bladder was a great favorite throughout Europe.) The Germans had their Mysteries and Passions—often concerned with Easter—but few Moralities. Instead they went in for the more secular entertainment of carnivals, which developed in the 15th century into the *Fastnachtsspiel* (see "Herr Sachs Sucks," page 46).

### Hee-haw

Ask your church to resurrect the Feast of Fools. It goes like this:

In December the local drunk would be elected King, or Pope, of Fools for a day. There would be drinking, general indecency, and a burlesque of the mass performed. At its close the "priest" would bray like a donkey and the congregation would reply "Hee-haw, Hee-haw, Hee-haw" (I wonder why a session in Congress springs to mind?). Despite popes' and bishops' attempts to ban the tradition, it lasted 400 years. A Jewish equivalent still exists.

**1478** When Piacenza is afflicted by persistent rain, the burial of a usurer in consecrated ground is blamed; the corpse is dug up, dragged around the streets, and deposited into the Po River.

**1485** Henry Tudor defeats King Richard III at the Battle of Bosworth.

**1492** Pope Innocent VIII, weak and in a coma, is given (probably orally) the blood of three young men, all of whom die—an early attempt at transfusion.

1470~1550

# Theater? What Theater?

## Machiavelli and the Italian Renaissance

*In theatrical terms the invention of printing has a lot to answer for. Take the Italians. Before the Renaissance they were having as much fun on stage as anyone, with a thriving diversity of strong local cultures, dialects, and artistic expression. Then some humanist scholars, with clearly not enough to do, discovered some Greek and Roman texts ("Hey look, guys, Classics!"). And the newfangled printing press meant that everyone got a text for Christmas.*

**Behind the Scenes**

Movable scenery brings many new theatrical possibilities.

No one knows for sure where and when the first Italian theater building was built. Nor is it known when the Italians started using scenery and what it looked like. What is known is that the Renaissance marked a hugely influential change from the rough outdoor medieval stage to purpose-built indoor theaters, perspective sets, and the beginnings of changeable scenery. Playwrights sat up and took note, but did this perhaps coincide with the unionization of stagehands?

The "Hall of Perspective" in Rome. A likely venue for adaptations of classical plays and general fooling around.

**1520** Elaborate, costly scenery and costumes and fantastic interludes dominate the drama in Italy; in Spain the Inquisition quells the spirit of dramatic invention.

**1521** Tribal divisions and internal strife allow Hernán Cortés to defeat the Aztec empire, which extends from central Mexico to Guatemala.

**1541** Michelangelo completes the *Last Judgment* in the Sistine Chapel.

First, in 1470, they printed an edition of Terence's plays, and two years later those of Plautus. Then they read Aristotle's *Poetics*, which made them all feel funny, after which they would speak only in Latin! So it came to pass that the dead hand of classical imitation gripped and froze the production of 15th-century tragedies (as well as its audiences). Some jokers claim that these scholars' pretentious adaptations didn't even warrant the name "theater." Finally, as if all this wasn't bad enough, someone thought it would be even cooler to sing the classics instead and as loudly as possible; thus was opera born.

Machiavelli thinking of a screamingly funny comic plot.

Happily, this wasn't the case with comedies. Although these too were drawn from aforesaid Roman and Greek models, the Italian comic writers were naturally gifted at improvisation and healthily cavalier about slavish translations. So the comedies developed well. There was the *commedia erudita*, a literary comedy of witty banter played by amateurs to socially exclusive courts. The best of these included *Il Marescalco* (*The Stablemaster*, 1527), by *Pietro* ARETINO (1492–1556), and *La Mandragola* (1518), by *Niccolò* MACHIAVELLI (1469–1527). (Never thought of *him* writing comedies, did you?) *La Mandragola* was very much a Renaissance play, mixing classical and indigenous folk material and characters to good effect. Then there was the very famous and popular commedia dell'arte acted by professionals, to great acclaim (see pages 26–7). There was also a third branch of the comedy, even more rustic, in the work of certain dramatists who made use of local dialects and peasant character types. The most notable among actor/dramatists of this genre are Andrea Calmo and Angelo Beolco—who was better known as Ruzzante, a name he took from one of his characters—and it is to these truly popular theatermakers that modern performers like Dario Fo have looked for inspiration (see page 123).

**School Plays**

Remember the school play with horror? Well, blame the Italians; they started it! (Actually, the tradition really began in 12th-century England, but it took off in 16th-century Italy during the age of the Reformation.) So, in the name of spiritual enlightenment and morality for young boys, Protestants staged anti-papist plays, Jesuits counterattacked with anti-Protestant plays, and both promoted anti-Semitism.

**c. 1500** The discovery of Greek sculpture (which had lost its color) and Roman sculpture (which had never been colored) influenced a move away from polychrome medieval figures.

**1533** Catherine de' Medici introduces the *bain marie* (double boiler) to the French court; its Italian name (*bagno maria*) recalls the legendary alchemist Maria de Cleofa.

**1560–74** Italian writer, painter, and architect Giorgio Vasari designs the Uffizi Palace in Florence, his most significant architectural work.

1500~1720

# Slapstick, Dirty Old Men, and Cuckolds

## The Italian *Commedia dell'arte*

*The brilliant commedia dell'arte ("comedy of the profession") began in northern Italy in the mid-16th century. Its usual material was improvised comic attacks on greed, lust, and status, performed on portable booth-stages that could be set up quickly indoors or out. Performers wore emblematic costumes and masks to represent stock characters. As Europe's first fully-fledged professional drama, it traveled across many borders in one form or another for over 200 years.*

Part of the reason it was able to do this was its vigorous visual and physical form of comedy based on traditional situations and stereotyped characters. It owed nothing to written scripting, preferring instead the "scenario," a sort of plot summary learned by the actors beforehand. These scenarios formed a skeletal structure on which to hang a huge variety of sketches and comic business that seemed more universal than local, and thus universally popular. Peter Brook (see page 137) would have felt right at home.

**Behind the Scenes**

An enduring element of the commedia was its stock characters, each with their own half masks and costumes. So, for example, a long nose and beard identified Pantalone, while Arlecchino wore a patched costume, which eventually became the diamond-pattern harlequin suit. He also carried a slapstick, two flat pieces of wood fixed at the handle which "slapped" loudly when he used the device to hit someone.

On one side, commedia characters included a group of tricksters comprising two low-status male clowns, or *zanni*, the stupid but hungry Arlecchino (Harlequin), and the crafty Brighella. On the other were two old fools, a lecherous trader, Pantalone,

**1600** Observing two children playing with lenses in his shop leads Dutch spectacle maker Hans Lippershey to invent the telescope.

**1692** One of the last outbreaks of witch-hunting occurs in Salem, Massachusetts, and 20 people are executed.

**1720** After losing his provincial inheritance, Pierre Marivaux embarks on a successful career as a dramatist with *Arlequin poli par l'amour* at the Théâtre Italien in Paris.

## Supporting Roles

*The traveling commedia players influenced all of Europe, especially France and Spain. In fact, their residencies in Paris at the Hôtel de Bourgogne were so successful the place was renamed Hôtel des Comédiens Italiens ordinaires du Roi, and the French had to call their comedy the* Comédie Française *to distinguish it from the* Comédie Italienne. *For 14 years, from 1658, Molière shared the same theater with the Italians.*

and Il Dottore, a weak and pedantic academic. One of these two often had a daughter or young wife called Isabella. In addition there were two lovers (various names), a bragging soldier, Capitano, and a smart and witty serving wench, Columbine.

The scenarios generally involved the tricksters trying to get their hands on the money/daughter of the old fools, and the stock-in-trade was vulgarity, bawdiness, and sexual innuendo. They perfected many examples of *lazzo* (comic devices) and *burla* (practical jokes). Traditionally the characters spoke jargon gibberish suitable for their roles as soldier, academic, or whatever. (Arlecchino spoke comic gibberish anyway.) The commedia troupes were the first to put women on the stage on equal (sometimes more favorable) terms with men. The roots of the commedia are unknown. Some have tried to link it to the Roman farces 1,500 years earlier, but although there are superficial resemblances, commedia is much more complex. A more probable antecedent is the clowning, acrobatics, patter, dancing, and singing that had always been a part of popular entertainment.

**Vulgarity**

Sexual vulgarity has been a very basic ingredient of theater probably from the beginning and, until the 16th century, was acceptable to both court and common society. It is found in rituals and performances all over the world to this day. For example, the Cherokee Indians, in their Booger dance, pad their bottoms and stomachs, wear phalluses, and take names like Black Buttocks, Rusty Anus, and Big Testicles. (So that's where all those old heavy-metal rockers got it from.)

Harlequin and Scaramouche in the hands of Roman cab drivers. A scene from the comedy *La Foire St. Germain*, from 1695.

**1486** Columbus persuades Ferdinand and Isabella of Spain to back his plan for a westward expedition; previous appeals to Portugal, France, and England have failed.

**1492** Luis de Torres and Rodrigo de Jerez report seeing natives "drinking smoke" in the New World; Rodrigo will later be imprisoned by the Spanish Inquisition for his "devilish habit" of smoking.

**1499** Fernando de Rojas' novel in dialogue *La Celestina (Tragicomedia de Calisto y Melibea)* combines romance, everyday life, obscenity, and entertainment.

1472~1650

# Golden Age of Spain

## Cervantes, de Vega, Calderón

An exorcism of a so-called bad woman. She was probably just a bad actress, but who can blame her tormentors? Painting by Lucas y Padilla.

*Spain's drama in the 16th century developed at a pace as rapid as that of its politics and fortunes. It grew out of the same medieval roots as the rest of Europe—religious yet a teensy bit profane. Spain of course had a strong Catholic church that was never what you might call liberal-minded ("No one expects the Spanish Inquisition"). But as long as actors stayed on the right side of heresy (wave your phallus about by all means but never claim to hear voices, o.k.?), they were allowed to continue.*

There are texts from 1472 (e.g., *A Dialogue between Love and an Old Man*, by Rodrigo Cota) written in the vernacular (i.e., not Latin). Of interest is the notorious and successful *Celestina*, also by Cota. This bold, frequently obscene and moralizing romance went through 30 editions from 1499 and was translated into French, German, Dutch, English, and Italian. Unlike the Italians, the Spaniards sensibly avoided trying to duplicate the "classics" of Greece and Rome. Writers like

**Behind the Scenes**

Spain developed rectangular theaters (modeled on courtyards—as opposed to the English circular ones based on bear-baiting rings). The principal Spanish theater in the 16th century was the Corral de la Cruz in Madrid. Like its English counterparts it had a three-level stage with trap doors, a gallery, balcony, and rear inner stage, and was open to the elements (though with a canvas covering against the heat of the sun). Plays started in the late afternoon (after a good lunch and a bit of a siesta— how civilized!), and audiences either stood in the pit or sat in the surrounding tiers to watch the action.

**1536** When Henry VIII dissolves the monasteries, England begins to suffer from a honey shortage; the monks had kept bees to provide wax for their votive candles.

**1577** El Greco, born in Crete and trained in Italy, settles in Toledo; his paintings uniquely blend these three influences.

**1630** Tirso de Molina's play *El Burlador de Savilla* is based on the legend of Don Juan; the story will be used subsequently by Molière, Mozart, and Lord Byron.

**OK Corral**

A corral theater was discovered and restored in the 1950s at Amalgro. Although its age is unknown, a pack of 17th-century cards was found in a rear dressing room (actors were obviously no more overworked then than now). This corral has three little balconies and a women's gallery (the *cazuela*, or "stewpan"—no comment!), because, unlike London, Spain considered mixing of the sexes far too licentious. Or was it that Spaniards were just terrified of women?

Encina, Torres Naharro, and Gil Vicente (who was actually Portuguese) gained fame in courts with their *comedias* (plays about the nobility, clergy, and their servants) and *autos sacramentales* (religious plays). Torres Naharro's works were savage and satirical about the court and the church and consequently were banned by the Inquisition. He fled to Naples, never to return.

Cervantes reading reviews of his first play. Before turning to writing, he'd been captured by Barbary pirates and wounded fighting Ottoman Turks.

*Miguel Cervantes* (1547–1616) (he of *Don Quixote* fame) tried his hand at dramas, but achieved little success. It wasn't until the magnificent talent of *Lope de Vega* (1562–1635) arrived that Spain's place on the theatrical map was ensured. A direct contemporary of Shakespeare, he perfected the three-act drama where action was more important than character sketches. He is said to have written 1,500 dramas in his life (an exaggeration, surely, since only 314 are agreed to be his. Many lesser writers liked to use his credit-worthy name). Among his most famous works are *The Idiot Lady* (1613), *Madrid Spa* (1602–12), and *The Dog in the Manger* (1613–15). After de Vega came the other great Spanish Golden Age writer *Pedro Calderón de la Barca* (1600–81). Between 1629 and 1640 he wrote his best comedies, tragedies, historical dramas, and autos, including *La Vida es sueño* (*Life Is a Dream*, 1635) and *La Cena del rey Baltasar* (*Belshazzar's Feast*, 1632).

Lope de Vega.

**1547** Any able-bodied person in England who does not work may be branded with a V for Vagrant and be obliged to work as a slave for two years.

**1549** The First Prayer Book of Edward VI is published; this and a second book in 1552, composed chiefly by Archbishop Cranmer, will strongly influence English prose style.

**1555** Richard Chancellor and others found the Muscovy Company (the Association of Merchant Adventurers), the first of the great English trading companies, to trade with Russia.

1485~1603

# Tudor Days

## Ralph Roister Doister to Gorboduc

Elizabeth I loved a good masque.

*From the 14th century onward virtually all of the European monarchs loved to prance around in masks and costumes whenever there wasn't a war on; goes with the job, I suppose. The Tudor kings were no different. Whenever a dignitary arrived at the court of Henry VIII, for example, theatrical Disguisings (wearing of masks and costumes) took place, with the monarch at the center of things.*

**Serial Killers**

*Gorboduc* had a great blood 'n' guts story line. The younger son of a king kills his brother, whereupon his mother kills him. The people revolt and kill both king and queen. The nobles kill the rebels—and then kill each other over succession to the crown. Unfortunately, however, all action happened offstage and was relayed only by messengers reeling off hundred-line speeches. Definitely must have been written by lawyers.

These events were amateur, but tons of money was spent on them and they were prepared with as much professionalism as any play. (Of course they were—everyone knew how Henry reacted when he was displeased!) So the Tudor court enjoyed spectacles where costume and sets were lavish but there was no story (except their own magnificence). But in the schools and universities, where some Greek and Latin was studied (despite the Reformation, during which anything Italian was Not a Good Thing), stories began to appear.

While the Italians had made absurdly pompous versions of the Roman classical texts of Terence and Plautus, and the Spaniards had sensibly avoided them, one or two English writers gave it a try with better success, even realizing their comic

**1556** Nuremberg shoemaker Hans Sachs's play *Der Paur im Egfeur* dramatizes anecdotes and everyday incidents; Sachs will appear as a character in Wagner's *Die Meistersinger von Nürnberg*.

**1559** Ice cream is made in Italy after it is discovered that ice and salt make a freezing combination.

**1562** English navigator John Hawkins hijacks a Portuguese ship carrying African slaves to Brazil and makes a huge profit when he trades his human cargo at Hispaniola.

potential arguably better than had the originals. An Eton schoolmaster, *Nicholas UDALL* (1504–56), penned a Roman-inspired rowdy comedy, *Ralph Roister Doister*, in 1550. Later, around 1560, a Cambridge art master, William Stevenson, wrote the more homely *Gammer Gurton's Needle*. This latter play has proved more enduring, as witnessed by various minor productions up to the 20th century. It is written in rhymed doggerel and concerns comic gossip and upheaval in a village over the loss of Gammer Gurton's needle. Surely this text is due for a new revival, preferably by British dramatist Steven Berkoff?

Not all plays of the time were a series of jolly japes. Four years after the coronation of that most vain, capricious, tightfisted, wily, brilliant, and nationalistic redhead, Elizabeth I (who did so much to promote the "Great Age" of English theater—although not financially, I hasten to add; not a chance!), a tragedy, written after the style of Seneca, appeared. The play, *Gorboduc*, was a joint venture between two young lawyers, *Thomas SACKVILLE* (1536–1608) and Thomas Norton. It was first performed to the queen *et. al.*, and, although dull, it was in English and blank verse to boot, and was thus instrumental in establishing the five-act form for tragedy later pursued by Marlowe and Shakespeare (see pages 32–5).

## Supporting Roles

*The professional actor was gaining ground during the 16th century, usually under royal or noble patronage (which helped protect one against the vagaries of politics or religious prejudice). Henry VII had four players in his employ; Henry VIII doubled the number. So, by the time the great plays came along in Elizabeth's reign, there was a pool of talent ready and waiting to act them. Actors were still regarded as lowlifes, however. It was illegal to challenge an actor to a duel, for example, because those in his profession were not considered to be gentlemen. If a gentleman became an actor, then he lost his gentlemanly status.*

Elizabeth I on the way to the theater. Some of her bearers have spotted an agent, and one has forgotten his panty hose.

**1552** Italian anatomist Bartolommeo Eustachio's *Tabulae Anatomicae* describes what will be called the Eustachian tube (in the ear) and the Eustachian valve (of the heart).

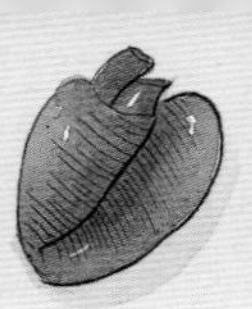

**1558** After 211 years of English rule, the French channel port of Calais falls to François, duc de Guise.

**1563** Protestant martyrologist John Foxe's *Actes and Monuments* is published in English; popularly known as *The Book of Martyrs*, it is inaccurate, partisan, naive, and vivid.

1550~1625

# The Glory Days

## The Burbages, Marlowe, Jonson

Christopher Marlowe, looking remarkably healthy for a guy with such a dissolute lifestyle.

*The years of Elizabeth's reign saw an incredible burst of theatrical energy, interest, and talent. About one in eight Londoners regularly went to watch performances of Marlowe, Shakespeare, Jonson, and others, a rate only matched by cinema around 1925–39. Arguably this was the last time in England during which theater was a truly communal activity in which audiences were respected and their esthetics and expectations matched on stage. It has since loftily elevated itself ever further from its public.*

One likely lad, a carpenter, *James BURBAGE* (c.1530–97) (also an actor with Lord Leicester's men), reckoned that there might be a good living in owning a purpose-built public theater. So, in 1576, his open-air playhouse, known as "the Theater," was built at Shoreditch (outside the city walls, since the Puritans weren't terribly keen on these "chapels of Satan"). He was right, and by 1600 the Curtain, Rose, Swan, Globe, and Fortune were all doing good business. His son, Richard, became one of the best, and best-known, actors of Shakespeare's great roles.

**Clever Witt**

If it hadn't been for the doodles of a Dutch tourist we wouldn't have much pictorial evidence of the Elizabethan stage. Johannes de Witt, a traveler visiting London in 1597, wrote in his diary about the theaters he had seen. He also made a drawing of the interior of the Swan. This was very helpful of him, because there are only three other (inferior) drawings of London theaters of the time.

*Christopher MARLOWE* (1564–93) had a typically Elizabethan, short, and violent life, dying at 29, knifed in mysterious circumstances. He was also reportedly a spy, a flamboyant homosexual, and an

**1581** Francis Drake seizes the Spanish treasure ship *Cacafuego* off Panama.

**1595** English poet Edmund Spenser on the plight of the Irish after Elizabeth I's forces have subjugated Ireland: "they looked like anatomies of death; they did eat the dead carrion."

**1597** English satirical pamphleteer Thomas Nashe and Ben Jonson cowrite *The Isle of Dogs*; it provokes a storm of outrage and all London theaters are closed.

outspoken atheist (a true rock star of the 16th century). Though wild and often drunk, he left us some of the most passionate poetic dialogue and sharpest characters ever created (like most Elizabethan writers, he ignored Seneca's classical unities). *Tamburlaine the Great* (1587), though not his first play, established his name. *The Jew of Malta* (1589), *Edward II* (1592), and *Doctor Faustus* (first edition dated 1604) followed. *Faustus*, with its searing dialogue and human pact with the Devil, is the most enduring.

**Live Hard, Die Young**

Artistic wild living was clearly de rigueur. Thomas Kyd (author of *The Spanish Tragedy*) was violent and blasphemous. He was imprisoned and tortured and died aged 35. The actor Robert Greene left his wife, spent his "marriage-money," called Shakespeare rude names, then died at 34 after too much "pickled herringe and Rennish wine." George Peel, (who wrote *The Old Wives' Tale*), though regularly drunk and dissolute, just made it to 40. "Eat, drink and be merry, for tomorrow we'll all be hanged."

*Ben* J*ONSON* (1572–1637), who amazingly *didn't* die young (though many wanted him to), has been called "Shakespeare's nearest rival." Gung ho radicalism landed him in jail more than once (he even killed another actor in a duel, receiving a branded thumb as punishment). A friend of Shakespeare (enemy of almost everyone else), he annotated the 1632 folio edition of the Bard's works with the words "He was not of an age, but for all time!" Jonson's main remembered works are *Every Man in His Humour* (1598), *Volpone* (1605), *The Alchemist* (1610), and *Bartholomew Fair* (1614). Some of Jonson's best writing, though, can be found in the masques he cocreated with his friend Inigo Jones (see pages 38–9).

**Behind the Scenes**

Two types of theater appeared at the same time, i.e., 1576: outdoor (such as the Globe) and indoor (for example, Blackfriars). The former were public and ideal for the technically simple plays of Shakespeare, Marlowe, and co. The latter, although called "private," were also public but cost more and attracted a snootier audience to watch, mainly, child actors, Jacobean tragedies, and masques. I know where I'd rather have been.

A modern performance of *Volpone* with Michael Gambon playing the title role.

**1573** An Italian adaptation of Euripides' *Phoenissae* is translated into English by G. Gascoigne and F. Kinwelmarshe; *Jocasta* is the first Greek tragedy in English.

**1578** The authorities describe Cambridge University as a "storehouse" for "prodigall, wastfull, ryotous, unlerned and insufficient persons."

**1580–1600** Leading English miniaturist Nicholas Hilliard develops a linear style and uses flesh tones rather than shadows to model faces in his portraits.

1564~1616

# And Now . . . the Man Himself

## William Shakespeare

*Ironically, more is known about others of the time than about the man himself. This is partly because others were better self-publicists (Greene, Jonson) or troublemakers (just about everyone); Shakespeare was neither. In fact, it seems he was a remarkably stable fellow.*

Will entreating fellow actors to stick to the words as he's written them.

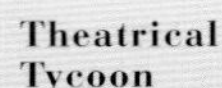

### Theatrical Tycoon

Philip Henslowe (died c.1616), an entrepreneur, pawnbroker, and theater owner, did as much as Burbage to consolidate theater-going. He owned the Rose, then the Fortune (in competition with Shakespeare's Globe), and, in 1614, he built the Hope Theater at Bankside to house both plays and animal baiting. He had several actors and writers under contract and used their debts to prevent them from leaving. He also encouraged the trademark of Jacobean drama: collaboration in writing plays.

In addition to writing, he acted and was later a partner in the Globe, a combination that made him rich as well as famous. Yet he kept his head down and warranted only about 50 mentions in print, with hardly any relating to theater. What's more, the only existing examples of his handwriting are six signatures, with four different spellings! Elizabethan plays tended not to get published because the author thereby sold his rights to the company who produced his work. So authors would only publish if they needed the cash. Copyright then meant that if you owned a copy of a play you had the right to produce it!

### Behind the Scenes

The theater that Shakespeare wrote for was technically a simple affair. It was a wide, planked, thrust stage on which there might have been some furniture, some simple mechanics but virtually no representational scenery, and surrounded by audience for 300°. It is no accident that the best theater throughout history has been achieved with the simplest of means—powerful images, words of conviction, and respect for the audience. (Good actors and a responsive house do, of course, help.)

**1589** Elizabeth I refuses to grant a patent for William Lee's knitting machine because it will deprive poor people of employment, so he sets up his invention in Rouen, France.

**1592** Drunkard and debtor Robert Greene publishes a fictionalized account of his deathbed repentance of his sins.

**1608** John Dee, English mathematician and astrologer, dies; his stage effects for Aristophanes' *Peace* gave him the reputation of being a magician.

### Flaming Set

If ever you find yourself complaining about fire regulations in theaters, don't! On June 29, 1613, during the first performance of *Henry VIII*, a cannon, fired as a special effect, set fire to the thatched roof. The great "Wooden O" was reduced to a pile of ashes within an hour. Funnily enough, they built the new Globe of 1614 with a tiled roof.

By the age of 28 he was already acting in the tragedies of Marlowe and *Thomas KYD* (1558–94), and had written *Henry V* (the first of 18 plays published during his lifetime), and he was certainly well known enough for another actor, *Robert GREENE* (1558–92), to jealously call him "an upstart Crow, beautified with our feathers." In 1594, by which time he had written three of his comedies and two tragedies, he joined The Lord Chamberlain's Men at the Theater of James Burbage, probably the best acting company. He was to stay with them for 20 years.

Playwriting didn't make good money (which is why so many writers ended up in prison for debt). It is therefore reasonable to suggest that Shakespeare owed a lot of his success to his association with Burbage, who was generous enough to grant him not only an actor's salary, but also a share of the profits (Burbage was no fool—"keep this clever kid sweet"). Such financial security meant he could write the material he wanted, rather than potboilers or collaborations. He thus churned out only about two texts a season (which is not bad going by today's standards—especially not if they were *Hamlet* and *King Lear*—but less than his contemporaries).

### Kids on Stage

The very popular "children's companies" were formed during the reign of Henry VIII, from chapel chorister boys. The most famous were the Children of the Royal Chapel and the Boys of St. Paul's. During the 1590s they were ousted by the adult, professional actors (or is that a contradiction in terms?), but returned around 1599 to the newly refurbished Blackfriars theater.

"I told you what would happen if you didn't brush your teeth." Scene from *Henry V*, Act V, painted c.1875.

**1603** A female attendant at the Izumo shrine in Japan leads a performance on a dry riverbed, which becomes known as *kabuki*.

**1609** Johannes Kepler publishes his laws of planetary motion, explaining that planets move in ellipses and get faster as they get closer to the Sun.

**1614** The Globe Theater is rebuilt, but 30 years later it is destroyed by the Puritans and does not reopen until 1996.

1603~1625

# Blood and Madness

## The Jolly Jacobeans

*Things certainly changed after Elizabeth shuffled off this mortal coil in 1603. Indecision, especially about a successor, and dottiness marked her last days. After the optimistic 1590s, a more moribund pessimism set in, heightened by the new monarch, charmless and snobby James I.*

Moreover, the writings of Machiavelli and Montaigne promoted a new, almost psychological, view of man as he really is—warts and all—and it wasn't pretty. All the certainties of a hierarchical order to the universe inherited from the Middle Ages were gone. This was reflected in theater. Revenge tragedy, where bad guys get what's coming, had been around since the Greeks, but it became meat and drink to the Jacobeans. (There were also masques: see pages 38–9.)

"If *you* had these boots on, *you'd* stand like this." *The Revenger's Tragedy* (1969 production).

### Supporting Roles

*Two other names to flourish in this era were* **Philip Massinger** *(1583–1640) and* **John Ford** *(1586–after 1639). Massinger's most famous work is* A New Way to Pay Old Debts *(1621), featuring well-known rascal Sir Giles Overreach, while Ford's output included the often revived* 'Tis Pity She's a Whore *(1626).*

Jacobean revenge tragedy conveyed a sense of the world as a "deep pit of darkness," by way of black humor, rough language, images of disease and dissolution, and overtones of stark staring madness, and pleasingly allowed for someone to get it in the neck (these days we have soap operas). *John Webster* (c.1578–c.1632) was the gloomiest of an altogether pretty

**1617** English traveler Fynes Morison's Itinerary records that Italian women "in many places weare silk or linnen breeches under their gownes" at a time when Englishwomen did not.

**1620** 102 Pilgrims leave Plymouth in the *Mayflower*, bound for Cape Cod; these English separatists have already emigrated to Holland but have now obtained a patent to settle in America.

**1624** Belgian physician and chemist Jan Baptista van Helmont introduces the term "gas"; he is the first scientist to distinguish between air and gases.

gloomy bunch writing for a rich and privileged few (who could afford to get depressed) in private indoor theaters. His two most powerful plays, *The White Devil* (1611) and *The Duchess of Malfi* (1613), share Italian settings and that ol' fascination with evil and death (and a bit of incest in case you got bored). Others were *John MARSTON* (?1575–1634), author of *The Malcontent* (1604), and *Cyril TOURNEUR* (?1575–1626) who (most likely) penned *The Revenger's Tragedy* (1607).

Everyone was also collaborating. Some even say Shakespeare cowrote *Henry VIII* with *John FLETCHER* (1579–1625). Fletcher more regularly collaborated with *Francis BEAUMONT* (1584–1616) on several plays, including *The Woman Hater* (1607) and *The Maid's Tragedy* (1611). *Thomas MIDDLETON* (1580–1627) (who might have been the author of *The Revenger's Tragedy*) collaborated with *Thomas ROWLEY* (?1585–1626) on *The Changeling* (1621), but he also wrote *Women Beware Women* (1612) and *A Chaste Maid in Cheapside* (1630) all by himself.

During the second decade of the 17th century the gloominess dispersed somewhat and everyone got all romantic, particularly Thomas Dekker (especially in *The Witch of Edmonton*, 1621) and Thomas Heywood (read *The English Traveller*, 1627). The latter work was marked more by compassion, sentiment, and melancholy than by the dark, violent visions of Webster.

### War of Words

The revival of the children's companies at the turn of the century provided an ideal and very popular cast for the private theaters. Public theaters were spurred to competition, satire dominated the playhouses, and what has been called the "War of the Theaters" broke out, in which playwright railed against playwright, openly insulting each other in their works. Sounds fun. And very creative.

### The Juvenals

A measure of the change in spirit was the rise, and fall, of satirical writing. As a reaction to the gentility of Elizabethan philosophy, a new breed of poets emerged. Joseph Hall, John Marston, and John Donne wrote caustic, truculent, and critical poems and pamphlets.

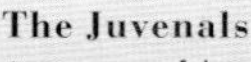

They were known as the Juvenals, and though the public loved them the church burned their works at the "bishops' bonfire" of 1599. Obviously as tolerant as ever.

"Come on, fair's fair. It's my turn for the wig now." Scene from *The White Devils* (National Theater).

**1606** The first open-air opera is produced in Rome

**1609-10** Ben Jonson's play *The Silent Woman* satirizes the merchant's wife: "All her teeth were made in Blackfriars, both her eyebrows in the Strand and her hair in Silver Street."

**1610** Galileo discovers the four moons of Jupiter through the newly invented telescope. He calls them the "Medicean Stars."

1605~1634

# Masque Makers to the Gentry

## Jones and Jonson

*Here is a time when expensive scenic design reached incredible heights in the masque, a courtly entertainment that, although possessing a solid text, was less of a play and more of an incredibly well-illustrated story. It was usually acted by dancers and singers, aided by the monarchy and assorted hangers-on.*

It had originated in pre-Christian folk customs and myths, and combined poetry, music, dance, fantastic costumes, and spectacular stage machinery that "permitted rocks to expand to mountain size, and trees to grow." As a court entertainment, it was an import from Renaissance Italy, and it went straight to the heart of the English and French aristocracy. (In England it was especially patronized by two Stuart queens, Anne and Henrietta.) Ben Jonson, that bad boy jailbird, almost had an alternative career as England's greatest writer of masques, collaborating with the brilliant architect and designer *Inigo JONES* (1573–1652).

While a student of architecture, Jones had traveled to Italy and become inspired by the Italian architect Palladio and the scenic designer Guiglio Parigi. After his return in 1605 he began to revolutionize the (indoor) stage, developing two-dimensional "cut-out" scenes in relief. By the late 1630s he had a fully operational system of flat wings in grooves, which slid out to reveal different scenes. In just 35 years he had achieved a feat that took the Italians a century.

An Inigo Jones costume, probably for a stock character known as the "daughter of the river Niger."

**Behind the Scenes**
Probably the greatest contribution of the masque to the history of theater was its promotion of Italianate scenery and stage machines. As well as reviving the Greek *periaktoi*, a three-sided machine with a different scene painted on each side, Jones added a *scena versatilis* (a two-sided swiveling front piece with a scene on each side), side shutters, and colored lighting by having candles behind bottles filled with colored liquid. Ingenious, huh?

**1612** English dramatist Thomas Heywood's *An Apology for Actors* is the best contemporary summary of traditional arguments defending the stage.

**1614** Scottish mathematician John Napier publishes the first table of logarithms.

**1630** In Japan, two families develop Kikkoman soy sauce; *kikko* is the Japanese word for tortoise shell and the hexagonal pattern on tortoise shells becomes the brand's trademark.

Masques were performed at Twelfth Night and other celebratory dates, initially in the banqueting hall of Whitehall Palace. Typical of the genre was *The Masque of Blackness* suggested by Queen Anne, who wished to appear as an African to her court! Dutifully, Jones and Jonson concocted a story about some "daughters of the river Niger" who were traveling the world seeking a cure for their blackness in order to become beautiful! For *The Masque of Queens* (1609) Jonson added a new ingredient, an antimasque, a grotesque or comic foil to the serious action in the drama. The intention was to provide contrast or balance to the events.

To Inigo Jones, the masque was essentially a vehicle for spectacular display. However, to Ben Jonson it was a dramatic poem based upon classical scholarship, and he often chided Jones for too much pomp and spectacle at the cost of the drama. Eventually, in 1634, they fell out irrevocably and the masque declined both in quality and in favor.

### Big Spenders

The cost of some masques was amazing. Ben Jonson's *The Masque of Oberon* cost £1,500, about three times the cost of building the Fortune theater the year before. James I, a man not known for generosity, once spent £4,000 on a single production of another masque. Today's equivalent would be about £250,000 (nearly $400,000), or the cost of a "think tank" for a modern opera house.

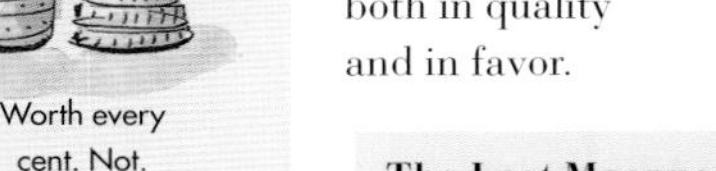

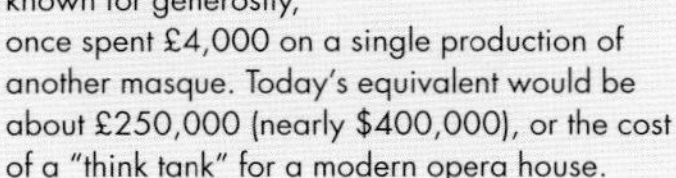

Worth every cent. Not.

### The Last Masques

The masque declined during the reign of Charles I, and both king and genre died out with the English Civil War. Watching dainty courtiers in fancy dress wasn't Cromwell's most favorite entertainment (unless they were heading toward the scaffold). The last masque before the Puritans became revolting was *Salmacida Spolia* by Inigo Jones (1640). It featured a violent storm in which Fury invokes "evil spirits to bring discord throughout England." Do you think he knew something?

"Do you think we've overdone things a bit this time?" A masque in the Bonner Hoftheater.

**1563** The Anglican Church is established, using dogma that is largely Protestant and a hierarchy like that of the Catholic Church.

**1602** Various Dutch companies trading with Indonesia amalgamate to form the Dutch East India Company, which will drive Portugal out of the spice trade within ten years.

**1648** Approximately 1,000,000 black slaves have been shipped from Africa to the New World.

1550~1700

# Big Noses and Bad Manners

## The Renaissance in France

*In 1548 the Paris Parlement banned Mystery plays, stifling a popular voice of political protest. From being its co-originator and patron, the Catholic Church became drama's enemy. For a century French actors weren't allowed a church burial unless they renounced their profession. The Protestant Church in Germany was similarly unimpressed with theater.*

Rodrigo shows them the way to the Green Room in Corneille's *El Cid.*

There were some farces and moralities performed, but the Confrérie de la Passion (Confraternity of the Passion), which had been given a monopoly over all drama in Paris, restricted performances to their own theater, the Hôtel de Bourgogne. And when the voice of a common people is stopped, who steps in? That's right, it's those dull, academic, power-tripping minorities who never get out and have no friends. I mean the usual suspects like the Jesuits and the Humanists trying to either resurrect the language of the élite (Latin) or "classic" dramas of the Romans. If it's old, it must be safe, right?

Fortunately, in 1570, the Italians came to the rescue in the form of visiting commedia dell'arte troupes. And one dramatist at least, *Alexandre HARDY* (1560–1631), could recognize slapstick from slipshod. His comedies breathed a little life back into the French stage. However, it wasn't until 1634 that Cardinal Richelieu ended the monopoly of the Confrérie by bringing another company to Paris to the Marais theater.

One of the writers this company used was *Pierre CORNEILLE* (1606–84), a poet-dramatist and the creator of the brilliant

*Cyrano de Bergerac was outrageous. His last play,* Le Pédant joué, *at the Hôtel de Bourgogne, featured the pompous actor Montfleury as the pedagogue. Bergerac thought his performance so bad he ordered him not to act for a month. Montfleury ignored him, but the following night Bergerac returned to the theater and drove him from the stage at swordpoint. That's what I call Criticism. Montfleury? Non, merci.*

**1650** The minuet is introduced at the French court.

**1675** French courtesan Ninon de Lenclos, whose salon attracts the principal literary and political figures of her day, admits at 60 that she owes her beauty to cosmetic aid.

**1693** Louis XIV sets up a committee to devise the *romains du roi* typefaces for the Imprimerie Royale; they are the first to be designed with engraving rather than calligraphy in mind.

tragicomedy of love and revenge *Le Cid* (1637). The leading tragedian of his day, he wrote more than 30 plays, mostly in the Neoclassical style, including *Horace* (1640) and *Polyceute* (1643).

The principal French thespians to follow included *Cyrano de Bergerac* (1620–55), *Jean Racine* (1639–99), and, of course, Molière (see pages 42–3). Bergerac was more famous for his wordplay, swordplay, and long nose (all immortalized in Edmond Rostand's drama bearing his name) than for his plays.

Racine was undoubtedly a brilliant poet and tragedian, writing masterpieces such as *Andromaque* (1667), *Iphigénie* (1674), and *Phèdre* (1677). He wrote one comedy, *Les Plaideurs* (1668), but no one thinks it's very funny. By all accounts, he was also a rather nasty and ingratiating person. He wrote lyrical odes to Louis XIV (for reward) and generally pandered to the aristocracy. After the Académie Française, in an act of unbelievable stupidity, refused the dying Molière an academic chair because he wouldn't renounce acting, they offered it to Racine instead, who unhesitatingly accepted. ("All academics are jealous of artists." Discuss.)

### Controlling the Riffraff

The Confrérie had a lot of trouble maintaining their monopoly and spent much time chasing "illegal" actors and performers of all shapes and hues. Legitimate acrobats, rope dancers, and singers who appeared at fairs and medicine shows had an unreasonable habit of bursting into bits of tragedy, comedy, and farce when no one official was looking, and then running off before the authorities could say "I arrest you!"

Rostand's play *Cyrano de Bergerac* with Antony Sher (right) in the title role as the man with the big nose.

**1629** Mexico City is flooded with up to six feet of water and is described by one onlooker as resembling a shipwreck rather than a city.

**1635** A mail coach between London and Edinburgh provides Britain's first inland postal service.

**1653** Philippe Quinault is the first playwright known to have received a percentage of receipts rather than a lump sum for a production of *Les Rivales*.

1622~1673

# Molière the Great

## Innovative Social Comedy

*The best dramatist France has ever produced, and one of the best in theater history, MOLIÈRE (Jean-Baptiste Poquelin, 1622–73) was also a brilliant actor. And so loved has he been as an intrinsic part of French culture that during World War II French soldiers are known to have carried paperback editions of his works. Yet he lies in an unmarked grave. Slighted authority has a very long memory.*

Molière: as great as Shakespeare and a much better actor.

**Last Rights**

Ironically, Molière died on stage of a coughing fit while playing the title role in his last play, *L'Invalide imaginaire*. The all-forgiving church denied him the sacrament of Extreme Unction and stipulated that he be buried at night in unconsecrated ground (Jesus would probably have wept). However, thousands of his fans and friends processed by torchlight with his cortège. Did the clergy quake with fear, or just pour themselves another sherry?

Stagestruck as a boy, he eschewed careers in his father's upholstery business and in law to work with the amateur stage. His first attempts were not too successful and he ended up in a debtors' prison. He was fortunate in joining the Béjarts' company Les Enfants de Famille, led by the actor Charles Dufresne, who established precedents in small-scale theater practice to which any modern company is forever indebted. He stayed several years with this company, writing plays, e.g., *L'Étoudi* (*The*

**1654** The water for New York City comes from a well operated by hand; Tokyo has been supplied by an aqueduct since the 1640s.

**1670** Pierre Puget, charged with designing a fleet of new warships, is ordered by Louis XIV's chief minister to stop making his ships beautiful.

**c.1672** Charles II of England orders that judges should wear wigs in court, as is the practice in France.

*Blunderer*, 1653) and *Dépit amoureux* (*Lovers' Quarrel*, 1656), and acting. *Le Docteur amoureux* (*The Doctor in Love*, 1658) so impressed Louis XIV that he sponsored Molière from then on. In 1662, at the age of 40, he married the teenage Armande Béjart and wrote *L'École des femmes* (*The School for Wives*, 1662), a reflection on the incompatibility of youth and age and the role of women! The church accused him of immorality and his rivals pilloried him in their own second-rate works. Molière wiped the floor with them all in *La Critique de l'École des femmes* so thoroughly yet good-humoredly that Louis commissioned him to produce some royal entertainments and even became godfather to his first child in 1664. The following year his company at the Palais-Royal was awarded a regular salary from the crown.

However, it was not all easy going. Molière's savage attack on religious hypocrisy, *Tartuffe* (1664), was closed after its première at Versailles until a revised version was created. This was done in 1667 but the church still got the Parlement to ban it for two years. *Dom Juan* (1665) was likewise withdrawn, probably because of the favorable portrayal of its hero as freethinking and healthily cynical. Both of these works were very successful with the public, but as any zealot will tell you, "what do they know?" Truth has a habit of emerging long after the zealots have disappeared, as evidenced by the fact that Molière's work is admired and performed to this day!

**Behind the Scenes**

Like the English Elizabethan writers, Molière created his brilliant characters and situations aided only by superb acting, emblematic costumes, and personal props and dialogue designed to encourage strong movement and visual display. There was never any need for high-tech machinery and stage devices. His theater space was indoors, lit by candles, and had a pit and "boxes" at the side for the nobility.

A scene from *Tartuffe*: the old lecher stuffs his face. Inset: Felicity Kendal as the young ingénue in a 1991 production.

**1661** Covent Garden (the former convent garden of the abbey of Westminster, confiscated with other church properties in 1534) becomes London's produce and flower market.

**1663** Katherine Philips, the "matchless Orinda," is the first woman to have a play professionally produced on the London stage.

**1675** Charles II founds the Royal Observatory at Greenwich, with the aim of "finding the longitude of places for perfecting navigation and astronomy."

1660~1710

# Decadence and Women!

## Restoration Theater

*After the Stuarts reclaimed the English throne in 1660, a period of great acting and physical improvement in the theater followed. Charles II allowed Sir William D'AVENANT (1606–68) to set up the Duke of York's Company at the Salisbury Court Theater in 1660, and Thomas KILLIGREW (1657–1719) to establish The King's Men at the Theater Royal, which became the first Drury Lane theater (mention of which brings a tear to the thespian eye). These two companies were granted the monopoly by Royal Patent to be the only legitimate companies in England.*

### Fancy Dresses

Sumptuousness was the order of the day. It is said that the Duke of York and Earl of Oxford lent robes for plays and that Charles once lent out his coronation robes (somehow can't see Queen Elizabeth II doing that). Pepys wrote of Charles also donating £500 for 16 scarlet robes to be made for Killigrew's production of *Catiline*. If ya got it, flaunt it!

Nell Gwyn (1650–87) looking in need of some vitamin C. Painted by Peter Lely.

A high standard of acting was set, mainly by some of the ex-boy "actresses" (known as "squeaking Cleopatras") from the pre-Cromwell days, who were now in their forties. In 1660, one Margaret Hughes, the first actress, clambered up on stage to play in *Othello*. Then there was that redoubtable

**PROMPT BOX**

Italy, Spain, and France had been quite happy with women on stage for many years, but Englishmen held on to their misogyny. By 1664 there were many actresses available, but Killigrew, at his Theater Royal, mainly used them in salacious comedies. He also had girls of six or seven on stage to sing lewd songs.

**1677** In Mrs. Aphra Behn's comedy *The Rover*, a man appears dressed only in "his shirt and drawers" in an amorous scene, the equivalent of a female striptease.

**1698** Jeremy Collier's *A Short View of the Immorality and Profaneness of the English Stage* attacks English playwrights and accuses them of mocking the clergy.

**1710** "Plumpers," or small cork balls placed inside each cheek to fill out the hollows left by missing teeth, will be in use until the 1780s.

teenage orange seller, Nell Gwyn. Her playing of Florimel in John Dryden's *Secret Love* (1667) caused Samuel Pepys to comment interestingly that she had "the motions and carriage ... the most that I ever saw any man have." And he wasn't the only one: Charles II liked her so much that he made her one of his mistresses. Pepys also thought Thomas Betterton "the best actor in the world" (it's not recorded what he thought of *his* "motions and carriage," though he *did* write that the actor Edward Kynaston was "the loveliest lady that ever I saw." Hmmm.).

## Supporting Roles

*Restoration writing was notable for its rude comedies and the boozy womanizing of its writers. George Etherege's* Love in a Tub *(1664) and* She Wou'd if She Cou'd *(1668), William Wycherley's* The Country Wife *(1675), and William Congreve's* The Way of the World *(1700) are all typical comedies of (bad) manners. Thomas D'Urfey mostly wrote rude songs and jokes and probably wrote on washroom walls. If so, have these walls been preserved in ancestral homes? I think we should be told.*

Betterton's wife, Mary, was an actress, whom Cibber (see pages 66–67) thought was "without a Rival." Elizabeth Barry had trained with D'Avenant, who thought her acting was dull. However, an affair with John Wilmot, Earl of Rochester, worked wonders for her and turned her into the greatest tragic actress of the 17th century. Anne Bracegirdle was the opposite, a great comic actress whose private life was referred to as a "model of virtue," which I think means dull. The first professional woman writer, Aphra Behn, wrote coarser plays than the men, and penned her most notable creation, *The Rover*, in 1677.

Anne Bracegirdle in Aphra Behn's *Widow Ranter*.

**Behind the Scenes**

Restoration theaters, such as the Theater Royal and the Duke's Theater, were indoors, had a proscenium, flats and backdrops, a balcony, and a deep apron forestage. This forestage was used most of the time because the auditorium had only candles for light, which meant the rear stage was in semidarkness. Easy to get lost—or worse—back there.

**1484** Jacob Sprenger, Dominican Inquisitor of Cologne, and Heinrich Krömer publish *Malleus Maleficarum*, a textbook on the seeking out and punishment of witches.

**1509** The anonymous German prose narrative *Fortunatus* is concerned with the search for riches, a primary preoccupation of the age.

**1530** To defend the newly formed Lutheran churches from Charles V, Protestant states of the Holy Roman Empire form the League of Schmalkalden.

1450~1600

# Herr Sachs Sucks

## Teutonic Popular Theater

*These days Shrove Tuesday is marked by the odd pancake, but in 16th-century Germany, particularly Nuremberg, it was occasion for the biggest carnival of all. And at the center of it was the* Fastnachtsspiel *(carnival play).*

Springing from pre-Christian fertility rites, this knockabout theater retained some of its communal ritual form. Instead of disengaging the audience as modern drama does, it was an integral part of the revelries involving audience and performer alike in a comic, bawdy, and robust celebration of spring and the community. Instead of appealing to the intellect, it went straight for the guts and groin (sounds simply *marvelous*, darling). Existing totally within the framework of the carnival, it was probably perceived as little different from the other entertainments on offer. The actors stepped out from the crowd at the beginning, announced their short play (about subjects like avarice, gluttony, or infidelity), and performed it (with the audience taking part). At the end, they stepped back into the crowd and got on with some serious drinking. I suppose you could call it a sort of early version of punk rock.

### Smack on the Wrist

Some of the *Fastnachtsspiele*, especially the *Lügenmärchen* (or tall stories), had elements of social satire. They used the protective license of Shrovetide to turn their society ass over tit, as it were, and remind the townsfolk, who suffered the more outrageous stupidity and greed of aristocracy, church, and local government, that things need not always be as they are. Perhaps Sachs was in the pay of the local burghers.

The Meistersingers of Nuremberg preparing to deliver another thigh-slapping toe-tapper before the release of their latest album.

**1587** Thousands of Germans suffer insanity and death after eating bread made from rye infected with the ergot fungus; ergotism is endemic in the German states.

**1587** German author Johan Spies compiles his *Historia von D. Johann Fausten*; the Faust legend goes back to before 1540, but this is the first published version.

**1596** English poet Sir John Harington invents the water closet but people don't take to it and still prefer their chamber pots.

A favorite stock character was Pickleherring, who typified the earthy beer-swilling German jokester. At the center of things, he would often ridicule the local burghers who ruled the town. Occasionally Pickleherring and other country peasants were themselves the object of ridicule (they were never popular with townsfolk), and this would prompt some vigorous and untheatrical physical "debate" in the streets!

*Hans* SACHS (1494–1576) attempted to "improve" later *Fastnachtsspiel* plays. He was a cobbler turned writer, who wrote 6,000 dull middle-class moralizing dramas, all of them happily forgotten. He replaced much of the healthy smut and horseplay in the *Fastnachtsspiel* with humanism, folksiness, and versions of his own Lutheran religion (I bet he was welcome in the bar). He took over a deserted church in 1550 and turned it into the first indoor German theater building. And although his plays may have been forgotten, he wasn't. Both Goethe and Wagner celebrated his "Germanness," the latter immortalizing him in his opera *Die Meistersinger von Nürnberg*. He was probably a nice guy who always remembered his mother's birthday and was kind to lame stray dogs on the streets.

### *Supporting Roles*

**Hans Rosenplüt** *and* **Hans Folz** *(both roughly 1450–1515) wrote early* Fastnachtsspiele *(known as* Revuespiele*), which consisted of characters delivering comic monologues. The* Handlungsspiele *(plot-plays) of Hans Sachs were a little more similar to today's drama. But all this fun couldn't last. The Protestant Church abolished the pre-Lent carnival, while the Catholics developed* Schuldrama *(Latin school drama), and all people called Hans were banned from writing plays. Religion stepped in to spoil the fun, just as in France* *(see page 40)**.*

Some say the Green Man (center), a Fastnachtsspiel character, was an early precursor of Santa.

**1585** Jamaican ginger reaches Britain on a ship from the West Indies. It is the first spice from the Far East to have been grown successfully in the West, but won't be the last.

**1596** Everyone is trying to solve the problem of longitude. In Spain, King Philip III offers a reward of 1,000 crowns and the Dutch parliament offers 10,000 florins.

**1601** William Parry's account of Anthony Sherley's expedition to Persia contains the first mention of coffee; Sherley introduces coffee to London, where it sells for £5 an ounce.

1585~1650

# The Brits on Tour

## Browne, Kempe, and the "Englische Komödianten"

*Before the Thirty Years' War ended in 1648 the only professional actors in Germany were in touring companies, first from England, then France and Italy. The Brits had been touring Europe since about 1580, mainly to escape the plague that had closed many theaters at home.*

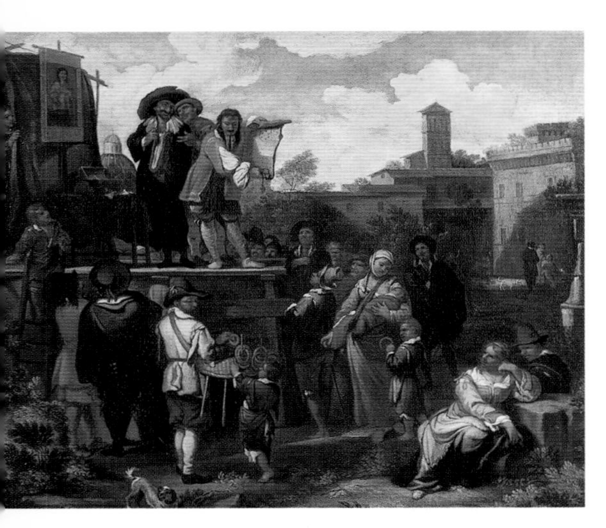

"It's no good showing them the script—they still won't get it." An early Brits tour.

Known as the Englische Komödianten (English Comedians), they enjoyed great prosperity and fame. One of the most important companies of Englische Komödianten was organized between 1592 and 1620 by Robert Browne, for whom Count Moritz of Hesse built a private theater in 1605 (see what I mean? In England he'd have been lucky to get a voiceover).

They had played to the Dutch and Danish courts in the late 1590s and appeared at Dresden. The famous Shakespearean clown *Will Kempe* (fl. 1600) often toured with other actors in the company of the Earl of Leicester. When in Germany, they enjoyed aristocratic patronage and many stayed behind to live a better thespian lifestyle.

As a repertoire they mostly produced home-country standards like *Gammer Gurton's Needle* (see page 31), comic sketches, and short biblical dramas, but they also included some mutilated clownish versions of Shakespeare and Marlowe (a tradition continued to this day at the Royal Shakespeare Company). In the early years

**1613** English sculptor of tomb monuments Nicolas Stone begins work in London; he is the most accomplished English sculptor of his day.

**1641** An ordinance of the English Parliament closes down public theaters in England "to appease and avert the wrath of God."

**1646** Charles I of England surrenders to the Scottish army at Newark; the following year the Scots will sell him to the English Parliament.

they acted in their native tongue, which would have necessitated performing in a very visual slapstick style, learning just enough Low German to get by. But later they added German actors and actresses and their shows began to be performed in the German language. However, the repertoire remained the same, which meant that German translations and new plays followed the same chopped-up "classic" texts and thus reproduced the same degree of coarseness, humor, and violence.

### Catholic Values

The most continuous theater tradition in Germany at this time was actually in the Jesuit colleges, mainly in Bavaria and Austria. Initial plays were in Latin (gradually replaced by vernacular) and intended to educate the boys in rhetoric and Catholic values. Performances favored spectacle and great musical scores, and may be seen as forerunners of the later spectacular operas of Germany and Bavaria. So that's where all the repression, guilt, and inhumanity comes from.

### Supporting Roles

*Of the few Germans who attempted to write a bit of quality for the stage,* **Jacob Ayrer, Andreas Gryphius,** *and* **Caspar von Lohenstein** *stand out. Ayrer wrote in the 16th century and none of his work has survived. Gryphius and von Lohenstein wrote 17th-century classical and baroque plays. However, their impact was minimal, since there weren't the companies to perform them. (Rather like the plight of the modern classical composer, then. One assumes they had day jobs.)*

The result was the *Haupt und Staatsaktionen*, German episodic texts, which mixed together copies of the English efforts with those of visiting Italian commedia dell'arte troupes. These plays seem to have relied on bombastic acting, gross obscenity, and lots of gore splashing around the stage. Sounds like good old thigh-slapping, Teutonic fun.

### Tour de France

After the Thirty Years' War ended in 1648, French companies and commedia troupes from Italy paid visits to Germany in droves. However, although the commedia plays went down well—Harlequin was a particular favorite—the plays of Corneille and Racine, and even those of Molière, made no impression. Germans were still happy to watch the slapstick antics of Pickleherring (what a hilarious guy he must have been).

Peter Brook's *Midsummer Night's Dream* in the 1970s—all Lycra and platforms.

**1592** Possibly the earliest written mention of a modern wig appears in the record of Henry VIII's privy purse expenses: 20 shillings "for a peryuke for Sexton, the king's fool."

**1600** Italian philosopher Giordano Bruno, condemned by the Inquisition for heresy, immoral conduct, and blasphemy, is burned at the stake.

**c.1650** Gianlorenzo Bernini creates his masterpiece *The Ecstasy of St. Teresa* for the Cornaro Chapel in the church of Santa Maria della Vittoria.

1590~1700

# Baroque? Actors Are Always Baroque!

## Italian *Melodramma* in Perspective

*If the commedia dell'arte represented one half of a culturally divided Italian society, then the* melodramma *(drama with music) and the scenic achievements accompanying it represented the other half. The origins of this form—which later came to be called opera—are confusing (just like opera itself).*

It is thought that the activities of the *camerate* (private clubs for scholars) formed after the Restoration, with their dramas of music and visual spectacle, together with the influence of the pastoral dramas (those idyllic "Shepherd Luvs Nymph Forever" poems of the Romans) had something to do with it. At any rate we might say both the *melodramma* and the commedia dell'arte are the greatest contributions Italy has made to the world stage. But only if we wanted to be rude.

Baroque theater is essentially about mind-boggling scenery and expensive sets (they had to distract attention from the weak scripts). Stage machinery was developed to feed the aristocratic taste for novelty. Clouds and whole

**Family Ties**

Commedia troupes liked to keep it in the family (a common Italian tendency). There were the Martinellis (Drusiano Martinelli was the first Arlecchino to visit England in 1577; his wife, Angelica Alberghini, ran the Uniti) and the Biancolellis, Francesco and Isabella, and their son, Giuseppe Domenico. Giovan Andreini came from another "family"; his parents, Francesco and Isabella, formed the Gelosi company before the Fedeli and . . . I hope you're taking notes..

Italian actors struggling to hang on to an audience who expected a more inspiring set.

**1663** English diarist Samuel Pepys notes the popularity of masks for ladies of fashion at the theater; "and so to the Exchange to buy a vizard (mask) for my wife."

**1670** Minute hands appear on watches for the first time.

**1698** French cellarer Dom Perignon pioneers the development of sparkling Champagne, decanting his wine made from a new blend of grapes into corked bottles of stout English glass.

## Supporting Roles

*Other commedia troupes of note were the* **Acessi**, *the* **Confidenti**, *and the* **Compaglia degli Uniti**. *The Acessi merged with the* **Fedeli** *and the Confidenti with the* **Uniti**. *All except the Uniti (problems of budget management, perhaps?) traveled abroad and all had ceased activities by the mid-1600s. However, commedia continued in less organized forms for another hundred years, and still influences Western theater. Old habits die hard.*

Arlecchino in full flight.

groups of "celestial" performers zoomed around on flying apparatuses, while sliding wing flats and shutters, painted with perspective-based designs, were fixed on to wheels to allow rapid scene changes. Special effects blossomed: birds sang, dragons breathed fire, cannons roared, chariots and ships crossed the stage, storms raged at sea, and cities burned. Practitioners like Alfonso Parigi (who *so* impressed Inigo Jones), Giovanni Aleotti, Giacomo Torelli, and Nicola Sabbatini dominated theater design throughout Europe. Torelli, in particular, is credited with the development of a system of wheels and rollers that allowed a single stagehand to move a whole range of flats and shutters at the same time.

There was also some tragic drama written in Italy during the 17th century, but fortunately very little. Probably just one writer emerged of any consequence—actor, company manager, and playwright *Giovan Battista* ANDREINI (1576/9–1654). Andreini made his name with *La Centaura*, 1622, and *Le Due commedie in commedia* (*Two Plays Within a Play*), 1623, which have occasionally been revived. Andreini was leader of the Fedeli ("the Faithful") troupe of commedia dell'arte players. Under the patronage of the duke of Mantua, the Fedeli created exotic court extravaganzas and traveled to the Hôtel de Bourgogne in Paris in 1614. Such exorbitance and splendor ... it's enough to give you the screaming vapors.

**Behind the Scenes**

Sabbatini left two volumes on theater design collectively titled *The Practice of Making Scenes and Machines*, 1637 and 1638. These were full of tips for stage technicians—not useful ones like "How to make your coffee break last two hours," but instructions on common requirements like "How to make dolphins and other sea monsters appear to spout water while swimming," and "How to divide the sky into sections."

Mezzetino receiving advice from his horse.

**c.400-500** The complex movements and expressions of Indian dance are integral to the drama of the period.

**500-600** Paintings reveal evidence of expertise in Indian textile-making, including pattern-weaving, and tie-dyeing.

**1000** Theater declines in India after the Muslim invasion, because the Muslims are opposed to drama.

?320~1920

# It's an *Epic*—Go to the Washroom First!

## India: Kalidasa and Shri-Harshadeva to Tagore

A scene from the *Ramayana*: "Wear this and your skin should return to normal."

*While rituals and myths in the West informed the development of theater, in India such rituals actually became the theater. From a time long before Christ, Indian drama followed three pathways: Sanskrit drama, which existed up to about* A.D. *1000, folk drama, and dance drama.*

Sanskrit drama is first referred to in the pre-Christian epic period, in those great (and *very, very* long) poems that detail all Indian culture, history, and religious beliefs, the *Mahabharata* and the *Ramayana*. The first dramatist was Bharata (*bharata* is now used to mean "actor"), though there are few details about him. He is said to have written the *Natyasastra*, a book laying out the form the drama was to take (Rule 1: It Shall Be Very Long). However, the most creative time was the Classic period, from about A.D. 100 to 800. Its two principal writers were Kalidasa and a king called Shudraka. Kalidasa created *Shakuntala* (*The Fatal Ring*), much admired by Goethe (mind you, he liked Pickleherring). Shudraka is credited with *The Little Clay*

**PROMPT BOX**

Dance drama was a silent form of speech, with actors' gestures and entire bodies "speaking" to an audience who, moreover, knew what they were saying. This theater has influenced Western visionaries like Brecht, Artaud, Brook, and Grotowsky. All the really major dudes, in fact, except perhaps Beckett (imagine *Krapp's Last Tape* as a silent, solo danc

**1526** Persianized Turkish invaders conquer the Delhi Sultanate and found the Mughal dynasty, which will rule most of India for over 200 years.

**1877** Queen Victoria is proclaimed the Empress of India with an ornate ceremony held in Delhi.

**1917** Rabindranath Tagore has Manipuri dancing taught at his school; the dance dramas Tagore writes for his pupils will help to overcome prejudice against Indian classical dancing.

**Behind the Scenes**

Bharata even dictated the staging of plays. Some were to be square, some oblong, and some even triangular. These theaters had a rear stage and a thrust apron with wings for actors' entrances. No one had to stand (unlike in the Globe, etc.) and seats were on a sloping platform "like a series of steps." There is mention of props and "machines" but no scenery.

*Cart*, a story about a poor merchant and a rich courtesan. Another king/writer, Shri-Harshadeva, reigned in the north between A.D. 607 and 647 and wrote *Ratnavali* (*The Pearl Necklace*), most notable for having a parrot as the central character (a tradition more recently revived by Monty Python).

The folk drama was a kind of popular play of improvisation, with characters and themes borrowed from the "classics." Any texts to survive are anonymous and research suggests they varied from performance to performance. In Indian dance drama the story line was an integral part of the experience, unlike Western dance, where it's all about how high you can leap in tights and silly dresses. One dance drama form, Kathakali from Kerala, has gained an international reputation right up to today. It has an unrestrained, bold, foot-stomping style with "superhuman" characterizations (the same guys who pop up in "Bollywood" movies from India) and blends dance, acting, and music. Unfortunately, not much of substance has survived from about A.D. 800 through to the works of Sir *Rabindranath TAGORE* (1861–1941), who wrote "eastern symbolist" and Neo-Romanticist plays such as *The King of the Dark Chamber*, 1914, and *The Cycle of Spring*, 1917.

## *Supporting Roles*

*Bhasa (4th or 5th century B.C.) has left 13 plays, of which* The Vision of Vasavadatta *is among the best Sanskrit dramas. Another writer, Bhavabuti (late 7th century), was known by his friends as "The Sweet Speaking" (oh really?). He penned the melodramatic* Malatimadhava *(or* The Stolen Marriage*), a Romeo-and-Juliet-alike except that the lovers get a happy ending.*

An Indian miniature based on the *Mahabharata*, the epic drama that chronicles the struggle between two rural families and the birth of the Indian nation.

**1191** Tendai monk Eisai attempts to restore pure Buddhism to Japan. Through his teachings, Zen will influence martial arts, Nō plays, poetry, flower arrangement, and the tea ceremony.

**c.1400-1500** Lakon drama dances are imported from Cambodia into Thailand; they are based on stories from a variety of sources and danced by women.

**1641** The Dutch capture Malacca from the Portuguese; the Dutch East India Company gains effective political control over the Malay archipelago.

800~today

# Wajang Gedog and the Shadows!

## Southeast Asia: Marionettes and Humans

Javanese dance drama.

*Several theatrical forms have flourished in Southeast Asia, the most prominent being the shadow play, the puppet play, and the dance drama. Stories are mythological, telling of the heroic battles of gods and kings against evil. In Burma a drama rather like that of India, and based on the* Ramayana, *has been recorded since the mid-18th century.*

There were also the *Nat-pwes* (god festivals), religious occasions where female mediums "acted out" the lives and decisions of dead gods (*nats*); these are performed in outside enclosures, with invited dignitaries sitting on platforms. (Good thing the Spanish Inquisition didn't know about *them*!) The main audience fills the enclosure and the stage is a series of mats. An orchestra is used, as are masks. Throughout Malaya and Thailand the shadow play and marionette performances have always been extremely popular.

Perhaps the most developed theater is in Indonesia, especially Java and Bali. Javanese theater falls into three basic forms: *wajang kulit* (shadow plays), *wajang topeng* (actors wearing masks and imitating puppets), and *wajang gedog* (pantomimic actors/dancers); *wajang* means "performance." The shadow plays are traceable at least as far back

**Behind the Scenes**
Audiences at shadow plays sit on both sides of the screen so some will see puppets and some will see the shadows they make. All the while, the gamelan plays its drums and gongs. These plays last throughout the night because it is thought any "malignant spirits" will have disappeared by dawn (if not, I find an Alka-Seltzer often does the trick).

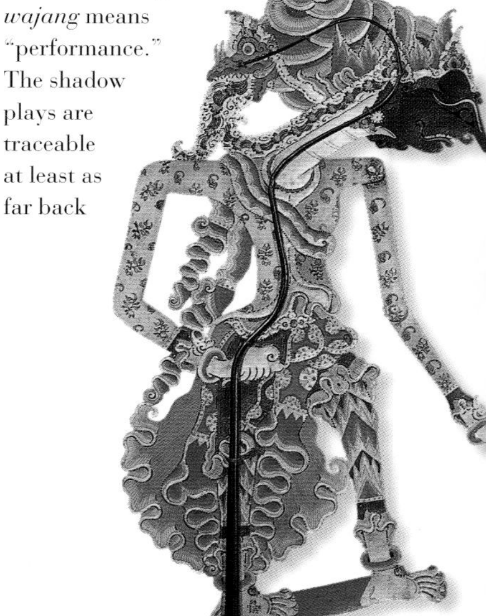

**1883** A volcanic eruption virtually destroys the island of Krakatau. Over 5,000 people die and the subsequent tidal wave kills more than 31,000 people in nearby Java and Sumatra.

**1953** New Zealand climber Edmund Hillary and his Sherpa guide make the first successful ascent of Mount Everest, the world's highest peak.

**1959** Tibet's Dalai Lama requests asylum in India after an unsuccessful rising against the Chinese garrison at Lhasa.

as the 7th century. In these performances, the grotesque, translucent leather puppets are manipulated behind a backlit white cloth by an invisible *dalang* (leader) who recites the performance, usually learned by heart. He moves the puppets by wooden rods attached to their thin arms (we stick our hands up the puppets' rear end; therein lies a Big Cultural Difference). He also directs the *gamelan*, or orchestra, who sit to the side of the performance space.

An Indonesian puppeteer: now you know why they are traditionally kept hidden from view.

In the *wajang topeng* performances, dancing actors hold masks to their faces by gripping a leather piece fixed inside the mask. This means they cannot speak, so, to avoid the "gottle o' gear" syndrome, their lines are chanted by another. This performance style is traceable to the 11th century and generally is based on Javanese versions of the *Ramayana* and *Mahabharata*, with additions in the Middle Ages of a new Javanese cycle of adventures known as *Panji*.

Rod puppets of the Sage Begawan Bisma and an (unhappy) maid, 19th century.

The *wajang gedog* actors perform without masks and in a pantomimic style. Initially this was a dance dumb show but Western influence has added speech. This new form is called the *wajang orang*. Plots are often melodramatic and concern the activities of hero figures, as in "How Petruk Becomes King of Madura." Like the other forms, these plays are performed in a building called a *pendoppo*, which is open on two sides.

**Trance Dance**

A Balinese specialty is the barong dance drama, usually known by tourists as the "trance dance." Performers pretend to be caught between two forces—the evil witch Rangda, and the good lion, the Barong, who tries to protect them (no, they don't go through a wardrobe first). It culminates in a frenzied trance during which performers roll on the floor trying to impale themselves on daggers—adding a literal dimension to the old theatrical expression "We died out there tonight!"

**200 B.C.** Stone chimes are among musical instruments used in China.

**140 B.C.** Caravans begin to carry "Chinese fruit" (apricots and peaches) to Europe, and grapes, pomegranates, and walnuts are introduced to China.

**444** The wheelbarrow is invented by the Chinese; during the period of the Six Dynasties they will also develop kites.

200 B.C.~1850

# Does Anyone Know What's Happening?

## Things Change Slowly in Chinese Theater

*Let's put your mind at rest . . . just in case you were worried. Basically, the Chinese theater has a form and tradition utterly incomprehensible to anyone in the West, so if that includes you, it's not your fault and you needn't be unduly embarrassed. Feel better now?*

From *The Sun and Moon.* They haven't figured out whose turn it is to shine.

**PROMPT BOX**

The Mongol emperor Kublai-Khan put a stop to intellectual Chinese writers getting cushy government jobs by "persuading" them (I don't think he was a man to refuse) to divert their creative energies to something more useful. Since he liked theater, they wrote plays, and lo! new stories about contemporary people gradually appeared.

Though a religious drama existed during the Hsia, Chou, and Tsin Dynasties (2000–200 B.C.), when actors were considered among the lowest life forms (when are they not?), the formal beginnings of Chinese theater were during the Tang Dynasty (A.D. 720–907), when puppet shows and music dramas flourished under the enlightened Emperor Ming Huang.

**550** In this century the Chinese invent gunpowder, which they use in fireworks.

**1230** Chen Ssu-tao writes the earliest known treatise on crickets, which are kept by the Chinese for their chirping.

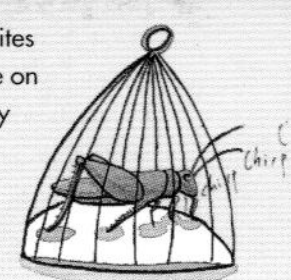


**1311** Paper money, in use by the Chinese since 1236, is discontinued when treasury reserves fail to keep up with the flood of currency.

He began a school for actors in his pear garden (actors are still called Pear Tree Garden Actors). Theater changed little in real terms from then to the 19th century, when Western influence entered the country. During the Song Dynasty (A.D. 960–1127), fully developed theaters, or *goulan*, appeared, the largest of which could hold thousands. Then, after the Mongols dropped by in 1234 to set up their Yuan Dynasty, the first great age of Chinese theater began.

The mask (later makeup) and costume we associate with Chinese theater dates roughly from this time. The main characters were the male, female, villain, and clown (the usual suspects). Makeup and costume are heavily symbolic; a white face means wickedness, a blue face means ferocious, a red face means courageous, a black veil means the actor is playing the dead ancestor of the hero, and a green face means the actor had a bad take-out meal the night before.

The first permanent playhouses were called "tea houses" and had a roofed thrust stage and balconies. The audience sat on three sides chatting, eating, drinking, playing games, and coming and going throughout the performance. You paid for the tea but the show was free.

The training of Chinese actors was famous (and very hard!). From childhood they would learn every single gesture in a character's "repertoire" for up to 200 fixed roles. From the start, women were trained just as the men were. This only stopped in the 18th century when, it is said, they got smart and began to marry nobility. This remained largely unchanged until the Cultural Revolution in 1949, after which it all got politically correct and boring.

**Crime Minister**

Confucius, he say: *"Man with big mouth not live long."*

One emperor loved heroic dramas that paid due reverence to his ancestors. Occasionally in need of a laugh, however, he would employ dwarfs and others to perform short comic pieces in which mild criticism of him and his court was encouraged. However, if the hapless actors criticized too much, Confucius (550–478 B.C.), in his role as Minister of Crime, had them executed. One of the situations, perhaps, where forgetting some of your lines might be the very best thing.

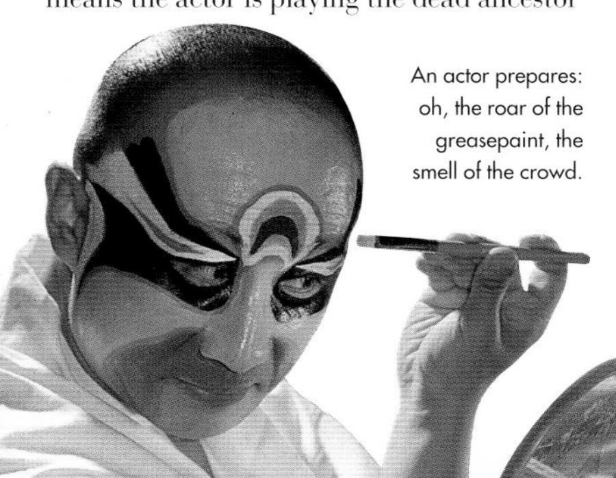

An actor prepares: oh, the roar of the greasepaint, the smell of the crowd.

**Behind the Scenes**

The Chinese stage has no scenery. Everything is implicit in the costume and gesture of the actor. For example, he mounts an imaginary horse by an exaggerated swing of his leg,and holds a wide sleeve between him and the other actors to disappear. The prop men who pile chairs and tables to symbolize a temple or boat, etc., wear black to indicate they are invisible (like funeral directors). And by the way, its always useful to know these things in advance.

**1300-1400** The aristocratic *nō* theater generates a new school of Japanese decorative textiles; the bold patterns of *nō* costumes represent a departure from Chinese textile design.

**1597** The warrior class in Japan represents eight percent of the population; in contemporary Europe it is no more that one percent.

**1637** The Japanese are said to "blow their Noses with a certaine sofft and tough kind of paper . . . which, having used, they Fling away as a Fillthy thing."

1200~the present

# No, No, Not No ... *Nō!*

## Monkey Music and Mannerism in Japan

*The Japanese theater must be the only place in the world where an actor dreams of being called* shite *(which means "first actor" in a* nō *drama) or, failing that, just* waki *(second actor). But enough of praise. This is also one of the few theaters still performing in a style that has remained largely unchanged for seven or eight hundred years. The aristocratic* nō *dramas reflect the Japanese tendency toward austerity of style and restrained, neat minimalist decorum—and once you're perfect, why bother to change it?*

Theater came to Japan from China via Korea around the end of the 6th century. The earliest performances were the pantomimic religious dances called *Kagura*, connected to Shinto worship. Japanese theater, like so much Asian theater, is inextricably linked to the religious and cultural makeup of the country. It is filled with dialogue, song, music, and dance and not pigeonholed, as it is in the West (with the exception of musicals and opera) into spoken word, music, or ballet, and so on.

**Behind the Scenes**
In addition to the stage, *kabuki* theater has the "flower way"—a walkway leading from the side of the stage to the back of the auditorium used for dramatic scenes. The revolving stage (an 18th-century Japanese invention) has trap doors, as does the "flower way," to allow actors to spring startlingly into view.

The *nō* ("art/skill") theater, with its comic sidekick *kyō gen* ("mad speech") theater came into existence some time in

The Japanese actor in stylized pose, costume, and lighting. Scary stuff! Solemn dances suggest the character's deepest emotions, in this case, disdain?

**c.1740** Limited color printing for the popular Ukiyo-E prints is introduced; previously prints were blocked and then hand colored.

**1798** London hatter John Hetherington makes the first top hat of silk shag, or plush, reducing demand for American beaver pelts.

**1953** When shellfish are polluted by methyl mercury, people in the Minamata Bay area of Japan suffer from worrying symptoms, sometimes followed by derangement and death.

the 12th century, patronized by the samurai classes and spiritually enriched by Zen Buddhism. *Nō* is a highly mannered form in which actors wear masks and move to music. The *kyō gen* were conceived as necessary parts of the theater structure (i.e., five *nō* need three *kyō gen* to stop everyone from getting too depressed). The

"I may have a smile on my face, but this is *nō* laughing matter."

**PROMPT BOX**

In full flow *kabuki* actors might whip off their costume to reveal another one underneath, burst into dance, or do some pantomime business that has nothing to do with the main plot. A Japanese critic wrote: "One might just as well climb a tree in quest of a fish as to expect logic and rationality in a *kabuki* play." Ah so!

most famous writer/performers of *nō* were *Kwanami* KIYOTSUGU (1333–84) and his son *Seami* MOTOKIYU (1363–1444). Seami developed the *sarrugaku* (monkey music—you know, three guitars and a drum kit), and was greatly revered.

*Kabuki*, however, was the punk rock of the 17th century. Started by a woman, O-Kuni, who went around soliciting funds for temples, *kabuki* filled the entertainment gap left by the aristocratic *nō* . With its rigid-faced, colorful actors moving like puppets, its scenery, wigs, and loads of costumes (a new one for each entrance), it proved very popular.

***Bunraku***

The puppet theater known as *bunraku* grew up around the same time as *kabuki* and continues today. Lifelike puppets with moving fingers, eyes, and mouth, manipulated by visible puppeteers, enact emotional stories that usually end in a ritual disemboweling or decapitation of a close relative.

**1708** Jean-François Regnard's play *Le Legataire Universel* has a valet as its central character, foreshadowing Beaumarchais' Figaro.

**1728** French dentist Pierre Fronchard makes false teeth using gold plate with teeth of jewelers' enamel.

**1765** Paris tavernkeeper Boulanger challenges the monopoly of the traiteurs and wins the right to serve a *restorante* (restorative) soup; the history of the restaurant starts here.

1700~1830

# Theater, Revolution, and Short Dictators

## 18th-Century France: Voltaire, Beaumarchais, Talma, and Napoleon

*In all fairness to the French, Molière and Corneille were hard acts to follow. But that doesn't entirely excuse the garbage passing off as theater during the 18th century. VOLTAIRE (François-Marie Arouet, 1694–1778) left off his dreary poems to have a stab at plays, but all he could manage were a few "classical," dull-but-worthy efforts.*

To make things worse, two new theater forms emerged which we could have done without: the lachrymose comedy and the bourgeois drama. The first were weepies, full of sentimental "hero-and-heroine-suffer-dreadfully-but-all-ends-well" sort of drivel. The second, initiated by Voltaire and *Denis DIDEROT* (1713–84), were middle-class dramas—sagas of everyday life (just what theater's best at, I don't think), serious in tone but with nauseatingly happy endings and moral lessons to be learned.

It wasn't until *BEAUMARCHAIS* (*Pierre-Augustin Caron*, 1732–99) appeared that Molière could stop spinning in his grave. This ex-watchmaker, secret agent, and gun-runner was undeniably a comic genius. His best known plays, *The Barber of Seville* (1775) and *The Marriage of Figaro* (1778), later turned into operas by Rossini and Mozart, were subversive in attacking the sacred cows of aristocratic society. In this he foresaw the Revolution, so both the plays and Beaumarchais were okay. Napoleon later called *The Marriage of Figaro* a "revolution already in action."

Voltaire dictating to his secretary while getting dressed. He must have had an important deadline to meet. Painting by Jean Huber.

**1784** Benjamin Franklin advises the French to set their clocks ahead one hour in spring and back one hour in the fall to take advantage of daylight.

**1806** Jean F. Chalgrin designs the Arc de Triomphe in Paris.

**1815** Allied soldiers passing through Épernay "liberate" 6,000 bottles of Champagne from the cellars of a M. Moët; the following year they will order—and pay for—the same quantity.

From *The Barber of Seville*. "Does Sir want a little something off the top?"

However, it has to be said that 18th-century French theater did produce some great actors/actresses. Adrienne Lecouvrer was by far the best actress at the Comédie Française, turning the most embarrassingly lurid dialogue into an intelligent, emotional tour de force (honest, she did; I was there ...). After her came Rachel, a young sensation who enticed Molière's best actor, Michel Baron, out of retirement at the age of 67. (He quit the stage at the height of his powers and no one seems to know why. They might reflect on the lines he had to utter.) Then, in 1743, Hippolyte Clairon demonstrated an amazing degree of control and ability to portray emotion without succumbing to it (yes, dear, it's called *acting*). Finally, the great François Talma shocked pompous Paris in his debut at the Comédie Française in 1787 dressed in a Roman toga with bare arms (saucy!).

In 1791, with support from Napoleon (who must have been taller than him), Talma opened the Théâtre de la République. Dictators are never too reliable, however, and 1804 saw Napoleon, who was never noted for his sense of proportion, introduce censorship (on reflection, maybe he knew what he was doing). Whereupon French theater fell into a hole for a few years.

**Party Poopers**

For someone who wrote crappy plays, Diderot at least knew what the experience of theater should be about. In 1758 he attacked the posting of guards in French theaters because of "rowdiness" in the pit. "Before," he lamented, "people arrived heatedly (and) went away in a state of drunkenness ... to brothels (or) polite society." "Now" the killjoys had made "theaters more peaceful and more respectful than churches." He wasn't at all keen on the church, and the attacks continued in his most important work, the influential *Encyclopédie*.

**Behind the Scenes**

The Revolution allowed any citizen to open up a theater for any type of drama. It also encouraged open-air festivals such as those organized by the painter Jacques-Louis David. A new audience, keen for spectacle, emerged. These crowds were part of the spectacle, not just observers. One of their favorite entertainments was the circus. Thus did the Franconi brothers prosper, opening their Cirque Olympique in 1807. Another highly popular spectacle of the period involved the decapitation of selected members of the aristocracy.

**1704** Antonio Vivaldi is established as a teacher at the Conservatorio dell'Ospedale della Pietà in Venice and will remain there until 1740.

**1718** A four-year war between Venice and Constantinople ends with the Treaty of Passarowitz; Venice retains only the Ionian Islands and the Dalmatian Coast.

**1764** Italian economist Cesare Bo'nesana condemns capital punishment and torture in his influential and widely translated *Tratto de delittie delle pene (On Crimes and Punishment).*

1700~1830

# Meanwhile, in Venice ...

## Papa Goldoni, Nasty Snr. Gozzi, and Alfieri

"Papa" Carlo Goldoni, painted by Alessandro Longhi. "Here's the table I write on."

*Unfortunately, before the end of the seventeenth century, Italy, like Germany, had come under the baleful influence of French theatrical ideas. But, although its best designers and actors had defected to Paris, all was not lost. A new theatrical form, opera buffa (comic opera—er... aren't they all?) appeared out of the Teatro dei Fioretini in Naples. Opera paid well, which must have been the only reason Venetian Carlo GOLDONI (1707–93), the first major Italian professional dramatist and brilliant reformer of comedy, wrote opera librettos between plays. After all, why do actors do commercials?*

Goldoni's plays basically brought together the spirit of the commedia dell'arte with the skills of playwriting. He wrote many different types of comedy, exploiting low and high, character and plot. His best works, such as *La Donna serpente* (*The Snake Woman*), *I Rusteghi* (*The Boors*, 1755), and *Arlecchino, servitore di due padroni* (*The Servant of Two Masters*, 1745), all demonstrate a highly developed sense of theatrical craftsmanship, a sharp social conscience in the satirizing of the upper classes, and clear respect for dialect and local character.

**A Natural**

One of Goldoni's problems in trying to breathe new life into the old commedia material was finding good enough actors. One such was Antonio Sacchi (1708–88), who played Arlecchino. Known as Truffaldino, Sacchi was an actor "people crowded to see." He could improvise on the maxims of Cicero and Montaigne, yet "ally them to the simplicity of the blockhead": a rare talent indeed. Not something learned at drama school.

He has been called the Italian Molière partly because he took the French writer as his model, but he never equaled him because he was far too nice to attack miscreant characters with the same joyful vitriol as Molière (he wasn't called Papa Goldoni for nothing; unfortunately niceness and posterity tend not to mix).

**1778** La Scala theater in Milan is built; it will be subsidized by season-ticket holders who will control its policies.

**1790** A meteorite shower falls in southwestern France; despite samples and 300 statements, the Académie Française declares the shower to be a "physically impossible phenomenon."

**1827** Italian poet and novelist Alessandro Manzoni finishes *I Promessi Sposi*; the novel, thought to be the greatest Italian prose work since Boccaccio, will not be published until 1840.

Alfieri, by Fabre. "I see Italians speaking quietly and sitting still. I must be ill."

The aristocratic *Count Carlo* G*OZZI* (1720–1806) hated Goldoni because of the latter's tampering with tradition, and his public criticism and carping finally drove Goldoni to Paris in 1762. Amazingly, Gozzi's dreadfully pretentious *Turandot* (1762) went over well throughout Europe, especially Germany (mind you, they would happily have stuck pins in their eyes as an alternative to snobby French Neoclassicism). He remained connected to the theater for just four years, after which he withdrew, grumbling and muttering about nasty changes in Italian life.

*Vittorio* A*LFIERI* (1749–1803) was the most esteemed serious Italian dramatist. His vision was of a more dignified and intellectually refined drama, classical yet modern in its nationalist flavor. He attempted to replace the excess and flamboyance of Italian acting with restraint and delicacy. He wasn't very successful; he might as well have been asking them to talk without moving their hands, and would have used his time far more effectively if he had relocated to Japan.

## Supporting Roles

*One good reason why hardly a decent play came out of 18th-century Italy is that most male playwrights used up all their energy between the bedsheets.* **Vincenzo Monti** *(1754–1828),* **Giovanni Pindemonte** *(1751–1812), and* **Niccolò Ugo Foscolo** *(1778–1827) were all more famous for their well-documented love lives than for their scribblings. Well, it's all a question of priorities, isn't it?*

**Behind the Scenes**

As the 18th century began, Venice had about 14 active theaters; by the beginning of the 19th, every city in Italy had at least one. Innovation in architecture, mechanical devices, and design in regular theaters (opera houses remained as sumptuous as ever) continued, but the ostentatious 17th-century extravagances began to be replaced by elements of delicacy and refinement. More naturalistic and rustic landscapes decorated the stage (production budgets were a bit thinner, perhaps).

Truffaldino in Gozzi's *The Love for Three Oranges*, ENO, 1989.

**1777** Frederick the Great declares, "It is disgusting to note the increase in the quantity of coffee used by my subjects . . . My people must drink beer."

**1782** Young German poet Schiller, having left his regiment without permission to attend a performance of his play *Die Räuber*, is arrested and condemned to write only medical treatises.

**1791–92** Poland defiantly proclaims a new constitution; by 1795 it will have disappeared from the map, absorbed by its three powerful neighbors, Russia, Prussia, and Austria.

1770~1830

# Sturm und Drang!

## Von Klinger, Goethe, and Schiller

*In the 1770s, several things happened which had far reaching long-term effects on German theater. Christoph Wieland's translations of Shakespeare into German achieved decent productions on the German stage; Rousseau's "natural" philosophy and Romanticism were given serious consideration; and finally, the American Revolution took place, which fired the imagination of anyone in Europe under the age of 30. One consequence of all this was that old Pickleherring was finally given the elbow and German theater began to think; a period of wild literary excitement ensued and passion made a dramatic entrance.*

*Goethe on the Ice*, by Maximilian von Brentano. While he oozes Sturm und Drang machismo, at least one of the ladies is a budding critic.

A group of Young Turks from Strassburg University, including the young Goethe, began an essentially Romantic movement dedicated to Shakespeare and all things "natural," "folksy," "primitive," "naïve," or in any way antienlightenment, antitradition, and antiauthority. They found a name for their artistic revolution in the title of a wild fantasy written in Shakespearean prose by *Friedrich Maximilian VON KLINGER* (1752–1831) called *Sturm und Drang* (*Storm and Stress*, 1776). Rebels and figures from mythology became dramatic heroes. Satan, Faust, and Prometheus all descended onto the stage to terrify audiences into the realization that humans were fallible, weak, yet potentially heroic—so a good time was guaranteed for all.

The acknowledged master of Sturm und Drang was *Johann Wolfgang VON GOETHE*

**1800** Romantic German poet Novalis (Friedrich von Hardenberg) publishes *Hymnen* and *Die Nacht;* he explores the death wish and symbolizes Romantic yearnings as "the blue flower."

**1814** Eau de Cologne becomes fashionable in England; originally called Aqua mirabilis, the perfumed water has been sold as a sideline by a firm of Italian silk dealers based in Cologne.

**1830** German chemist Justus von Liebig and U.S. chemist Samuel Guthrie independently discover the anesthetic properties of chloric ether, or chloroform.

(1749–1832). He had great ideas but was too untheatrical to write decent plays. His principal work, *Faust*, took from 1775 to 1832 to complete (and was published posthumously). An early version, *Urfaust*, was influenced by Hans Sachs's theatrical style. Goethe's *Faust* was different from Marlowe's in that while the latter wanted unlimited power, Goethe's sought inner understanding of the mystery of life. (That's progress.) He also wrote *Götz von Berlichingen* (1773), the story of a 16th-century Robin Hood-like robber, *Clavigo* (1774), *Stella* (1776), and umpteen novels and poems.

Schiller, painted just before he wrote *Don Carlos;* hence the dreamy expression.

### Working with Animals

Despite his love for them, there was one woman who nearly drove Goethe mad. He was manager of the Weimar Court Theater when the spoiled and demanding actress Karoline Jagemann arrived. She insisted that he put on *The Dog of Montargis*, a French nonsense that featured a poodle in the lead role. Goethe resigned his job in disgust. He obviously wasn't an animal lover.

*Friedrich von* SCHILLER (1759–1805) was a close friend of Goethe's, and, although Goethe wasn't always so friendly, the two influenced each other all their lives.

### PROMPT BOX

The play *Sturm und Drang* was originally to be called *Der Wirrwarr* (*The Hurly-Burly*). It was the odd Swiss writer Christoph Kaufmann who suggested the change and he clearly had the gift of foresight. Somehow a revolutionary literary and theater movement called Wirrwarr! or Hurly-Burly! doesn't have quite the same authority about it.

### Supporting Roles

*Writers of Sturm und Drang plays either went mad or gave it up for safer activities, like life. You think I'm joking?* **Jakob Lenz** *(1751–92) idolized Goethe to such an extent that he became a social embarrassment. Obviously very confused, he died in an asylum.* **Friedrich von Klinger** *left theater after a few years and ended up a general in the Russian army.*

Schiller's plays, *Die Räuber* (*The Robbers*, 1781), *Fiesco* (1783), and *Kabale und Liebe* (*Intrigue and Love*, 1784), were all Sturm und Drang plays full of passion, patriots, and avengers of the oppressed. Later he wrote *Don Carlos* (1787), a much quieter romantic drama of social change, followed by the *Wallenstein* trilogy (1799), giving Germany one of its most outstanding and durable stage characters. Coleridge liked *Wallenstein* so much, he translated it into English.

**1699–1712** Castle Howard, an imposing baroque mansion, is built in Yorkshire; its architect is English playwright Sir John Vanbrugh.

**1745** The British Excise Act taxes glass by weight; less lead is used in glass manufacture, and drinking glasses become smaller and more highly decorated, especially on the stem.

**1760** The Archbishop of Canterbury forces the Drury Lane Theater management to remove the line "You snub-nose son of a bitch" from the play *The Minor*.

1696~1815

# Handsome Rogues

## Cibber, Garrick, Sheridan, *et. al.*

Colley Cibber: "Hello, my darlings! Would anyone like this nose hair as a memento?"

*One 18th-century theater development was the amount of hot air in print by and about actors and managers. Reminiscences, criticism, and diaries proliferated from every thespian (and, methinks, every orifice). Colley* CIBBER *(1671–1757) penned* An Apology for the Life of Colley Cibber, Comedian *in 1740 ("apology" here means "account," though either meaning would do). This provided one of the most complete accounts ever written of the lot of the vain actor. Cibber began as a comic actor under Thomas Betterton at Drury Lane, wrote some mediocre plays, and became actor-manager at Drury Lane and the Haymarket. George II made him poet laureate. It pays to be a windbag (a useful tip to remember, I find).*

**Flouting the Law**

The Licencing Act of 1737, continuing the monopoly created by the Royal Patents in London, limited legal playhouses to Covent Garden, Drury Lane, and the Haymarket. It was engineered by the loathsome Sir Robert Walpole to censor writers like Henry Fielding, who, in his burlesque comedies, reminded the public of Walpole's corruption. The Act made all other theaters illegal, a status they blithely ignored. Bribes helped keep the local economies going.

In terms of acting, *David* GARRICK (1717–79) was simply the best, and he got everyone to agree with him. Samuel Johnson, James Boswell, and the painter Joshua Reynolds all adored Garrick in their memoirs. Garrick could act any character, was a dramatist, adapted Shakespeare, and dazzled London society with his brilliance, wit, and talent. There had never been anyone like him in English theater. As manager of Drury Lane (1747–76) he elevated theater to new heights of professional discipline (i.e., actors arrived on time and sober). If he'd had time, he'd probably have solved the

**1764** In protest at contemporary vulgarity, a group of young Englishmen form the Macaroni Club, where extreme sensibility and effeminacy in dress prevail.

**1773** The Royal Society gives Joseph Priestley a medal; through experimenting with the carbon dioxide produced by a neighboring brewery, he has invented soda water.

**1813** A Russian navy captain visiting Japanese stores sees prepackaged and prepriced goods—something as yet unknown in the West.

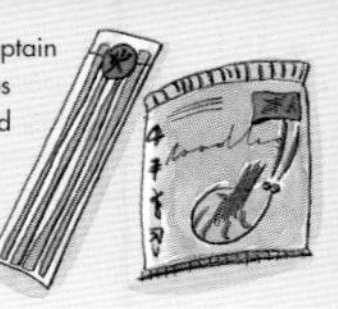

**PROMPT BOX**

The first Covent Garden Theater opened in 1732, thus sharing monopoly with Drury Lane, which itself enlarged in 1787 to 2,000 capacity, and to 3,600 at the end of the century. English theaters had no "stacks" of Italian boxes. Instead, balconies were spread wide and deep and walls fanned out from the stage to increase capacity and revenue. Thus did greed create bad sightlines and bellowing actors—and still does.

Mystery of Life (as it was, he just pioneered modern theater management).

Another handsome rogue was *Richard Brinsley SHERIDAN* (1751–1816), who wrote several brilliant comedies, including *The Rivals* (1775), *School for Scandal* (1777), and *The Critic; or A Tragedy Rehearsed* (1779); but he was more interested in political fame. Most of his resources were channeled into getting him into Parliament (the best show in town, after all). He bought the Drury Lane Theater in 1776 but didn't look after it, so it fell into disrepair and had to be rebuilt in 1791. It reopened in 1794 and, with the help of actors Mrs. Siddons and John Philip Kemble, it became a success.

It burned down in 1809, and Sheridan had to rebuild it again. This time, as it burned, Sheridan sat in a café across the street. When friends asked him what he was doing, he remonstrated, "Can a man not warm himself by his own fire?"

Actor *John Philip KEMBLE* (1757–1823) managed Drury Lane under Sheridan, and went on to Covent Garden, where his sister, *Sarah SIDDONS* (1755–1831), gave many a memorable performance. In 1808 Covent Garden burned down (careless back then, weren't they!), and after rebuilding it, Kemble and Siddons tried to recoup losses by raising admission prices. This provoked the "Old Price Riots," which devastated performances for three months.

## *Supporting Roles*

*John Gay (1685–1732) wrote* The Beggar's Opera *in 1728 (which inspired Bertolt Brecht to create* The Threepenny Opera *with music by Kurt Weill). Another theatrical Irishman was Robert Wilks, who was so loved in Ireland that the Lord Lieutenant issued a warrant to prevent his leaving the country. Oliver Goldsmith's* She Stoops to Conquer, *1773, is frequently revived today.*

Captain Macheath, the gallant highwayman two women fight over in *The Beggar's Opera.*

**1751** The young George Washington visits Barbados and samples its tropical fruit; "none pleases my taste as do's the pine [pineapple]".

**1764** Houses are numbered for the first time in London.

**1769** Spanish Franciscan Father Junipero Serra plants the first wine grapes, oranges, figs, and olives in California at the newly founded Mission of San Diego de Alcala.

1750~1815

# The Brits on Tour II: The United States

## Kean & Murray, Hallam, Fennell, and Cooper

*Due largely to the religious ideals of the Puritans and the Quakers, theater in the United States was rather slow in getting off the ground. So virtually all actors of note were English, French, or Italian tourists. This was a time when Puritan critics with funny names made the rules—people like "Increase Mather" (no sane person calls his son "Increase"; he in turn called his son Cotton), who complained of the "gynecandrical dancing" on stage.*

Not just an elaborate hunch: Thomas Kean's Richard III was said to carry the Drury Lane Theater.

In 1750, the Commonwealth of Massachusetts passed a law banning theatrical performances and their "painted vanities," while New England zealots billed *Othello* as "A Series of Moral Dialogues, in Five Parts, Depicting the Evils of Jealousy and Other Bad Passions." I blame it on chafing underwear.

Not all of the U.S. was so hostile. Virginia, Charleston, and Philadelphia, for example, had their own small theaters and provided a base for visiting English companies. Thomas Kean and William Murray toured a company to Philadelphia in 1749, and opened *Richard III* in New York in 1750 with Kean as Richard. The first well-organized company to visit the U.S. was made up of 12 English actors (who couldn't get jobs in England!), brought together by William Hallam. They opened at Williamsburg in 1752 with *The Merchant of Venice*. A year later they moved to New York. But as yet no real "stars" had visited the U.S., and didn't until the attitude began to perceptibly change toward the end of the century.

Kean "blacked up" to play Othello—and looking pretty ridiculous.

**1773** In protest against the British tax on tea, Bostonians board three British ships and empty their cargo of tea into Boston Harbor.

**1783** American lexicographer Noah Webster publishes his *American Spelling Book*, which will help to standardize American spelling. His *Dictionary* will be published in 1828.

**1803** Maryland farmer Thomas Moore patents the first icebox; it will be in common use by 1838.

The first "big name" to visit was an ex-Covent Garden tragedian, *James FENNELL* (1766–1816), who became an instant success on his arrival in Philadelphia in 1792, playing roles like Othello and Lear. He made a lot of money but invested it unwisely and, after a spell in prison for debt, died poor and mad (perhaps he was the first real Method actor). *Thomas Abthorpe COOPER* (1776–1849), although not as successful in London as Fennell had been, was considered excellent in his 1796 American debut as Macbeth at the Chestnut Street Theater in Philadelphia. He discarded the American stock system in favor of traveling from one company to another, performing only starring roles. In 1801 he moved to the Park Street Theater in New York and five years later joined its management.

## *Supporting Roles*

**George Frederick Cooke** *(1756–1811), star of Covent Garden in 1800–1803, specialized in meaty satanic roles like Richard III, Shylock, Iago, and Sir Giles Overreach. Widely considered to be Kemble's only serious rival, he might have gone on to even greater things had it not been for the demon alcohol. Cooper persuaded him to try his luck in the United States, and, when sober, he was apparently brilliant—though when drunk a liability, albeit an entertaining one.*

### What's in a Name?

Not surprisingly, when the Revolution became imminent, there was increasing antagonism toward English actors. Even the fact that David Douglass, after taking over from William Hallam, changed the name of the Company of London Comedians to the American Company of Comedians didn't impress the locals. By the 1770s, many states banned theater altogether and most English actors wisely scurried off to Jamaica.

Cooper as Richmond
(to Kean as Richard III): "Go on, admit it! My sideburns are better."

**1821** English actor Junius Brutus Booth goes to the United States to play Richard III in Richmond, Virginia, and settles there; one of his two actor sons will assassinate Abraham Lincoln.

**1827** Parisian students introduce the Mardi Gras (Shrove Tuesday) celebration to New Orleans.

**1832** The stage musical *Jim Crow* wins 20 encores at the City Theater in Louisville, Kentucky.

1815~1905

# The First Age of the American Actors

## Payne, Forrest, the Booths, and Those Barrymores

*When it did get going, American theater raced ahead. Plenty of good actors and actresses appeared and theater buildings increased from a mere handful in 1800 to five thousand by 1885. Good writers came later—evidence that the most fundamental element of any theater is the live presence of the actor (the live presence of an audience has also been known to help).*

**PROMPT BOX**

The American Minstrelsy Show, where white men mocked Negroes by blacking their faces and singing stupid songs, was popularized by Thomas D. Rice (1806–60). He introduced the "comic" Negro character Jim Crow to the stage. Despite its crass racism, "minstrelsy" continued up to the 1960s, with the televised "Black and White Minstrel Show" in Britain.

Thomas Rice as Jim Crow (Bowery, New York, 1833). Note "enlightened" all-white audience, crowds on stage (some fighting) and tacky backdrop.

John *Payne* (1791–1852) was the first American star. He also published the first American theater journal, *The Thespian Mirror*, in 1804, before he was 15 years old. (However, he had his off days, such as when he wrote the kitsch popular song "Home, Sweet Home.")

*Edwin Forrest* (1806–72) was the first American-born actor to achieve fame abroad. This "vast animal bewildered by a grain of genius" appeared at many of the finest American theaters before attempting to beat the English in their own backyard in 1836. The response was sneering contempt (the English treat foreigners, new ideas, and rabies alike), and the worst came from fellow thespians. Shaken but not deterred, he returned to the United States and went on to greater things.

**1861–65** The American Civil War will take more than 600,000 lives, destroy property worth $5 billion, buy freedom for four million slaves, and leave a legacy of bitterness in the South.

**1868** Alcatraz, an island off San Francisco, is first used as a prison. No one ever escapes and lives to tell the tale.

**1900** Mark Twain returns to the United States after ten years' absence; the *New York Times* hails him as "the Hero as Man of Letters."

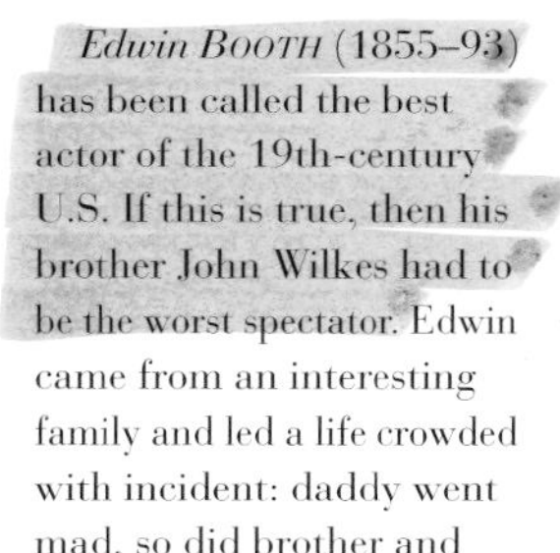

*Edwin* BOOTH (1855–93) has been called the best actor of the 19th-century U.S. If this is true, then his brother John Wilkes had to be the worst spectator. Edwin came from an interesting family and led a life crowded with incident: daddy went mad, so did brother and wife, other brother killed president, nephew killed someone else, Winter Garden (which he managed) burned down, and finally, he went bankrupt. After John Wilkes Booth shot Abraham Lincoln, the family got no more invitations to barbecues, so Edwin had to retire.

Booth as Hamlet (1864), looking for his brother in the balcony. He gave 100 consecutive performances.

In 1866 he ventured nervously back onstage, worried there might be someone like his brother out there. But before he had spoken a word, the audience burst into applause (they had either decided he was blameless or had reappraised Lincoln).

The Barrymore dynasty began with a Mrs. *DREW* (1820–97), who made tons of money managing the Arch Street Theater in Philadelphia. Her son John was a comedian and her daughter, Georgie, married Maurice Barrymore (real name Herbert Blythe). Their marriage produced Lionel, John, and Ethel, later called the "royal family of Broadway," all of whom started in stage classics and moved to film.

## *Supporting Roles*

**James Hackett** *(1800–71) played Falstaff to great acclaim in New York and in England.* **Robert Montgomery Bird** *(1806–54) won a thousand-dollar prize (offered by Edwin Forrest to stimulate American writing) with* The Gladiator *(1831).* **Ira Aldridge** *(1810–66) was one of the first African-American actors. He was valet to Edmund Kean and eventually played Othello in Russia and England.*

**1802** Mme. Tussaud's museum of waxworks opens in London; the Swiss wax modeler made death masks of famous guillotine victims in Paris during the Reign of Terror.

**1802** In London, only Covent Garden and Drury Lane theaters are licensed for the performance of drama; too large to permit subtlety and naturalism, they rely on spectacle and melodrama.

**1826** Louis-Jacques-Mandé Daguerre, who has been painting scenery for the Paris Opéra, approaches J. N. Niepce and proposes a partnership.

1800~1870

# Horrid Little Men

## Kean, Kemble, Vestris

*Edmund KEAN (1787–1833), later called genius, brilliant, etc., had a rather uninspiring start. His parentage is unknown but he was said to have had an "adventurous childhood." In 1807, he was described by his overbearing costar, Mrs. Siddons, as a "horrid little man" of whom there was "too little ... to make a great actor." Was she ever wrong!*

Edmund Kean playing Richard III at the Garrick Club, looking more like Ali Baba than the king of England.

Kean revolutionized acting by sudden transitions from "low" to "high" in his delivery, which is what Coleridge alluded to when he said watching Kean was like "reading Shakespeare by flashes of lightning." Later in his life these "flashes" dimmed as he succumbed to fame, booze, and sex. He burned himself out at age 44 (but what a life!). His son, Charles, was also an actor, but one with the charisma and talent of a fencepost.

*Charles KEMBLE* (1775–1854), younger brother of John Philip (also a thesp), was a handsome actor who managed Covent Garden. But he spent too much money, and his daughter, *Fanny KEMBLE* (1809–93), had to act (which she hated) to bail him out. *Lucia VESTRIS* (1797–1856) was a "breeches" actress, which means she played men's roles—a tradition extending in England to the "principal boy" in modern pantomime. She later managed the Olympic Theater.

**Behind the Scenes**

Lucia Vestris promoted the box set, probably a French import, with its realistic, "roomlike" setting containing real doors, furniture, and a ceiling instead of hanging "borders." She used these sets in her productions of Shakespeare's *Midsummer Night's Dream*, Boucicault's *London Assurance*, and Gay's *The Beggar's Opera*. Multiple sets also appeared, where several "rooms" were visible at the same time, a device used by the likes of Alan Ayckbourn in the 20th century (see page 121).

**Seeking the Limelight**

"Limelight" was a form of lighting beginning in 1816. A piece of limestone was heated with a mixture of gases and, when reflected by a mirror, became an intense spotlight. After 1860 the auditorium could be darkened and just the stage lit by using piped coal/gas, which could be extinguished and relit with electric sparks.

**1830** Irish inventor Aeneas Coffee patents the continuous still, which speeds up the distilling process for whisky and gin and produces a purer spirit.

**1847–48** Under the pseudonyms Currer, Ellis, and Acton Bell, the three Brontë sisters, Charlotte, Emily, and Anne, publish their first novels *Jane Eyre*, *Wuthering Heights*, and *Agnes Grey*.

**1848** Retired schoolteacher Dorothea Lynde Dix informs the U.S. Congress of over 9,000 epileptics and mentally ill persons who are being maltreated in insane asylums.

Before the monopoly of the patent theaters was abolished in 1843, "minor" theaters were permitted to put on pantomimic and musical shows. These had to comprise three acts only (five were for the "legitimate" playhouses) and could contain five or six songs but absolutely no spoken dialogue (from this we get the "musical"). However, dialogue crept in (in 1832 *Othello* was performed with an occasional plonk from a piano to make it legal), and, to compete with the successful "minor" theaters, Drury Lane and Covent Garden put on ever more spectacular shows. Ships exploded and sank, buildings burned, fire engines raced across the stage. Covent Garden once filled the entire stage area with water for *The Cataract of the Ganges*, and a cannon explosion at Drury Lane killed a member of the audience (hence the famous Drury Lane ghost).

## Supporting Roles

*This was also the time of the great clown* **Joseph Grimaldi** *(1779–1837), the "King of Clowns." Famous for his white makeup with two red half-moons on the cheeks, he was best known as Harlequin in* Mother Goose, *also performed as* The Golden Egg *(Covent Garden, 1806). His antics and talent became the benchmark for all clowns since, many of whom annually visit his Pentonville, London, grave to this day.*

In 1817, gaslight arrived on the stage. Conveyed by miles of rubber tubing, it could take controlled light to anywhere in the theater. However, the fumes accumulated beneath the roof, and viewers sitting in the "gods" sometimes fainted or even expired (theatergoers were so much more *dedicated* in those days). It also caused many fires; nearly 400 theaters burned down in the United States and Europe during the century.

Grimaldi in *The Red Dwarf*. After killing Pantaloon, he dresses him as Lion, Ass, Eagle, Cat, and Fish.

**1852–54** Isambard Kingdom Brunel and Sir Matthew Wyatt design Paddington Station in London; the structure combines glass and iron and has additional decorative details.

**1857** The Indian Mutiny begins when both Hindu and Muslim soldiers in the British army refuse to bite open greased rifle cartridges, believing them to be coated with taboo animal fat.

**1860** Boucicault's play *The Colleen Bawn, or the Brides of Garryowen,* premieres.

1850~1900

# The Actor and the Manager

## Macready, Phelps, Bancroft, Irving, Terry

*The 19th century saw a growth in Europe and the U.S. of the actor-manager of larger and more financially viable theaters. Yet hardly any decent plays were written. Experimentation, when it came later in the century, veered toward Naturalism and Realism, which were sweeping over Europe and the U.S.*

The hot-tempered *William MACREADY* (1793–1873) was an actor who managed Covent Garden before Lucia Vestris. He encouraged the poet Robert Browning and novelist Edward Bulwer-Lytton to write for the stage (but he really shouldn't have bothered). *Samuel PHELPS* (1804–78) took on the Sadler's Wells music hall in London, which had fallen into disrepair. He staged only melodramas by the best—Dion Boucicault and Tom Taylor, plus Elizabethan and Jacobean plays—and his approach turned the fortunes of Sadler's around. Lilian Baylis later used his example as a model for her revival of London's Old Vic.

**PROMPT BOX**

Ellen Terry allowed Henry Irving to dominate her career, something which so incensed George Bernard Shaw that he began a long and loving correspondence with her. Terry, unhappily married, had an illicit affair with the married architect E. W. Godwin that produced two children, one of whom was Edward Gordon Craig (see page 104), and one of her great nephews is Sir John Gielgud. So Irving did something useful.

Irving as Henry VIII. His elocution and gait were supposedly rather "mannered."

**In the Spotlight**

Henry Irving was such an egotist that he wanted to establish the Lyceum as a center of acting excellence—with himself as the most excellent. It is rumored that any lighting technician who did not focus the spotlight exclusively on Irving, even when he was standing to one side while another actor was speaking, was dismissed. I'm sure it's just a rumor. But in any case, what's the point of being the star if people can't see you shine?

**1883** English juries convict 12,000 people, while magistrates send 80,000 to jail without trial.

**1890** English soap manufacturer William Lever builds a Sunlight soap factory and creates the model industrial town of Port Sunlight.

**1900** English actress Mrs. Patrick Campbell appears in Frank Harris's *Mr. and Mrs. Daventry*, based on an idea purchased from Oscar Wilde, who dies in the same year.

*Sir Squire* BANCROFT (1841–1926), whose name sounds like a character in a Jacobean farce, his wife, Marie Wilton, and the playwright *Tom* ROBERTSON (1829–71), are all credited with the first development of Naturalism/Realism on the English stage.

W. S. Gilbert, a lawyer by training. "I am a doggerel bard" runs the refrain to one of his ballads.

Robertson's plays, *Ours* (1866), *Caste* (1867), and *School* (1869), produced by the Bancrofts at the Prince of Wales Theater, were all styled realistically in setting and language. Detractors dubbed them "cup-and-saucer" dramas (since Robertson had put real tea on stage; but, by the way, stage whisky is—yes, you've got it—real tea).

The bigwigs of the century were *Sir Henry* IRVING (1838–1905), the first actor to be knighted, and *Dame Ellen* TERRY (1874–1928). Irving ran the Lyceum from 1878 until his production of *Macbeth* in 1888, which failed and almost ruined him (not unlike Peter O'Toole in 1980—powerful stuff, that Scottish play). He was an egotistical actor whose only criterion in selecting the plays he wanted to show was whether they had terrific parts for him to play. On the other hand, Ellen Terry, whom Irving kept firmly in his shadow, was a genuinely marvelous actress.

### The D'Oyly Carte Company

"With some music and librettas, they produced their operettas. Even if they're mediocre, they earned lots of filthy lucre." See, it's easy! William Gilbert and Arthur Sullivan, together with Richard D'Oyly Carte, formed the D'Oyly Carte Company and created a series of silly operettas. After the success of *Trial by Jury* (1875) and *H. M. S. Pinafore* (1878) they produced 12 other crowd-pullers at the Savoy.

Arthur Sullivan. As well as operettas, he wrote the tune for the hymn "Onward Christian Soldiers."

### Supporting Roles

*It is said that the Irish-American* **Dion Boucicault** *invented the touring system per se. Arriving in the United States in 1853, he fought to protect the legal rights of authors. He achieved some basic "sole rights" for authors, reducing the theft of plays by actors/managers, and sent several companies on tour to act his plays without star performers, hence the "touring" system.*

The "well-made play" came largely from the pens of French writers *Eugène* SCRIBE (1791–1861) and *Victorien* SARDOU (1831–1908). Scribe wrote more than 350 plays. Originating in the comedy of intrigue, they were crafted to arouse suspense by starting with a detailed exposition of plot and then developing crises and complications before a climactic ending. It is a basic formula that has influenced theater in the West ever since.

**1835** Karl Schinkel, inspired by the medieval castles he has seen in England, builds the picturesque Schloss Babelsberg in Germany.

**1851** Franz Dingelstedt becomes director of the Munich Theater; his elaborate productions will make theatrical history.

**1862** Otto von Bismarck becomes Prussian premier; under his rule, Prussia will defeat Austria and take leadership over the newly created North German Confederation.

1830~1900

# Nationalism vs. Naturalism

## Büchner, Saxe-Meinengen, Wagner

Ibsen's *Ghosts* shocked contemporary audiences and set new standards in acting.

*Bored by the escapist ramblings of the Romantics, another group of young Germans tried to create a more dynamic, nationalistic theater, to take up where Sturm und Drang left off. They formed the Junges Deutschland (Young Germany) movement of the 1830s and 1840s. Unfortunately censorship and the dominance of the well-made play dampened their ardor.*

Of their writers, *Georg BÜCHNER* (1813–37) was considered one of the best. A revolutionary, he died of typhoid at 24. *Danton's Death* (1835), though brilliant, was never played in his lifetime. Neither was the portion of a work entitled *Woyzeck* (1836), which Alban Berg turned into an opera after World War I.

**PROMPT BOX**

The Freie Bühne was modeled on the French Théâtre-libre (see page 79), which also influenced Stanislavsky's Moscow Arts Theater. It was followed by the Freie Volksbühne (Free People's Stage) established by Bruno Wille in 1890. Wille went on to found the Neue Freie Bühne (New Free Stage) in 1892, which survived until 1933 despite many police and state attempts to close it.

*GEORGE II, Duke of Saxe-Meinengen* (1826–1914), unintentionally brought about one of the biggest changes in Western theater when he challenged the

**1876** The Reichsbank is opened; it will play an important role in German economic development.

**1895** Bavarian physicist Wilhelm Roentgen discovers X rays; it will now be possible to photograph the internal organs of animals and humans.

**1897-1900** Ferdinand Count von Zeppelin invents the first airship, or rigid-type dirigible balloon; the Zeppelin will be used by Germany in World War I.

dire German practice of "big" solo acting with crowd scenes played like wooden opera choruses. He introduced ensemble acting, "the collective personality of the group," which by default brought the stage director to the fore. The Meinengen Players visited nine countries between 1874 and 1890 and were seen by all the major figures in theater, some of whom, like Stanislavsky, were to develop these ideas further.

A self-styled "total man of the theater" and revolutionary, *Richard WAGNER* (1813–83) argued that theater should be *Gesamtkunstwerk*, or "total artwork."

Richard Wagner: his ideas, like his personality, were on a grand scale.

While this theory was undoubtedly brilliant and influenced the future direction of theater design, in practice it was only partly successful, since his staging tended always to be typical of "spectacle theater." His most famous work was the *Ring of the Nibelungs* cycle (1853–74). Wagner's opus has caused controversy since the first performances, and he has often been accused of violent anti-Semitism and vigorous pro-Nazism. Naturalism finally gained a hold in Germany with the so-called Freie Bühne, or "free stage," of Otto Brahm. Created as a subscription organization to avoid censorship by the police, who wouldn't allow the bourgeois to be offended (some things never change), it opened for business with Ibsen's *Ghosts* in 1889 and lasted for only three seasons. But it had set the German Naturalism revolution in motion, inspiring many imitators in its wake.

### Supporting Roles

**Heinrich Laube** *(1806–84) and* **Karl Gutzkow** *(1811–79) were the leaders of the Young Germany movement. Gutzkow wrote* Uriel Acosta *(1847), the seminal work of the group, reflecting its liberal sentiments. When he was imprisoned for "political offenses," Laube, who had also spent nine months in jail for openly supporting the French Revolution, turned against the movement. He later changed his allegiance and leaned to the right politically.*

**1830** Parisian M. Croisat revives the hairdressing profession by introducing the "1830 Mode," an elaborate style requiring professional skill.

**1840** French socialist Pierre Joseph Proudhon, in his treatise *Qu'est-ce que la propriété?*, declares that "Property is theft."

**1851** The majority of French people have endorsed by plebiscite the new constitution introduced by Louis Napoleon after his coup.

1830~1900

# Romanticism vs. Naturalism

## Hugo, de Musset, Sardou, Bernhardt, and Antoine

Victor Hugo photographed in 1875.

*It hardly seems possible to us now that the style of a stage play should cause a riot. But* Hernani *by Victor HUGO (1802–85) did. It opened at the Comédie Française in 1830 and upset the delicate French aesthetes in three ways: it scorned the classical unities, it contained popular theater devices, and, third, it was written by a man who was already despised as the leading Romantic and an antiestablishment political writer (something for everyone). He had previously set out the theoretical basis for Romantic drama in the preface to his play* Cromwell *(1827), claiming elements of the sublime and grotesque could be combined in the same play (Oh! The rascal!). Alfred DE MUSSET (1810–57), a better dramatist than Hugo, wrote to be read. But both dramatists reached the stage and have been revived many times since.*

**PROMPT BOX**

The great French actress Rachel was actually Swiss and her real name was Elisa Felix. As a child she was so poor she sang on the streets until she was 11, when the musician Alexandre Étienne Choron took her under his protection. She then went to the *Conservatoire* and thence to the Comédie.

The subject matter of the "well-made plays" of Eugène Scribe and Victorien Sardou (see page 75) was the bourgeoisie, while situation and "intrigue" tended to dominate character development. Bernard Shaw disliked them intensely, coining the rude epithet "Sardoodledum"—but he could be an old grouch, and made a career out of being cantankerous.

Nevertheless, the actress *Sarah BERNHARDT* (1844–1923) achieved her reputation in Sardou's plays at the Comédie Française, especially *Théodora* (1884). She also took the title role of de Musset's Shakespearean drama *Lorenzaccio* (written 1834) in 1896. From 1880 Bernhardt toured England, Denmark, Russia, North and South

**1858** The Bibliothèque Nationale (national library) opens to the public in Paris.

**1869** The butter substitute margarine is developed by French chemist Hippolyte Mège-Mouris. British dairy farmers try to get a bill passed requiring it to be colored purple.

**1900** Economic necessity forces French artist Henri Matisse to paint decorations for the Paris Exposition.

## *Supporting Roles*

*For the Romantics,* **Edmond Rostand** *(with* Cyrano de Bergerac, *1897—50 years after the Romantic movement had died) and* **Alexandre Dumas *père*** (Henry III and His Court, *1827). For the Realists/Naturalists,* **Alexandre Dumas *fils*** (Le Demi-monde, *1855),* **Émile Zola** (Thérèse Raquin, *1867),* **Henry Becque** (The Vultures, *1882), and the most "naturalistic" of all,* **Eugène Brieux** (The Red Robe, *1900).*

America, and Australia, then drove everyone nuts with endless "farewell" performances—the last few of which she performed after her leg had been amputated.

The person who probably did the most to advance Naturalism/Realism on the stage was a young Paris gas company clerk and amateur actor called *André ANTOINE* (1858–1943). In 1887 he rented a hall and began a "free" theater—the *Théâtre-libre*, a private playhouse open only to subscribers. For eight years he produced experimental playwrights who weren't granted productions elsewhere. He went further than Saxe-Meinengen, too, in making his actors speak and move as real people, sometimes having them speak lines with their backs to the audience. He used realistic settings with real food and everyday furniture. (Now theater can be as dull as being at home!)

### Crowd Trouble

For the opening night of *Hernani*, Victor Hugo (1802–85) dispensed with his paid claque of supporters, counting on the "artists of Paris," who loved him, to help. They turned out in velvet suits and floppy hats to combat the "classicists" who hissed and sang at the top of their voices. Then the fists flew. These days they might prefer a boxing match, although they would be advised to change their uniform.

### Going Bust

Although Antoine's Théâtre-libre had, by 1890, presented to the French the first performances of plays by Ibsen, Tolstoy, Strindberg, and Hauptmann and had over 12,000 articles written about it, it was in financial ruin. In 1894, unable to make a profit and owing some 100,000 francs, he turned it over to another director.

Sarah Bernhardt as Cleopatra: "This is my best side."

**1820** Italian author Alessandro Manzoni's historical verse tragedy *Carmagnola* completely disregards the Classical "unities"; he is the founder of Italian Romantic drama.

**1839** Naples and Portici are linked by the first Italian railroad, which covers a distance of five miles.

**1861** Lombardy, Piedmont, Modena, Lucca, Romagna, Tuscany, and the two Sicilies unite under Victor Emmanuel II of Piedmont to form the Kingdom of Italy; Venice and Rome will join later.

1820~1900

# Nationalism vs. Everyone in Italy

## D'Annunzio, Ristori, Duse, Salvini

*Italy had one major issue on its mind during the 19th century: becoming Italian. The struggle for unity and independence from the Bourbons, the Papal States, and the dreaded French Classicism preoccupied the aristocracy (working people, as always, weren't asked and anyway hadn't time to give a hoot about such things). So Italy's theater went uncharacteristically quiet.*

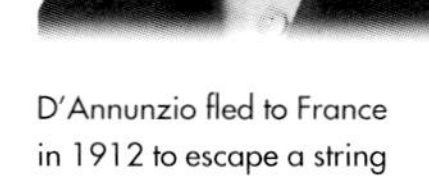

D'Annunzio fled to France in 1912 to escape a string of creditors who were anxious to talk to him.

When Romanticism arrived it was given a strong nationalistic flavor. Realism had to wait until Italy become a nation in 1870. The Italian version was called Verismo, but differed from French or German Realism in that the church was very powerful, and, Italian men being what they are anyway, there was no talk of women's rights, labor legislation, divorce, or liberalizing marriage laws. Heavens no, Italian Realism stuck to really important issues like preserving the lifestyles of the rich! Later, Naturalism appeared only in the north, while the south remained stubbornly feudalistic.

**PROMPT BOX**

D'Annunzio wasn't very generous to Eleonora Duse. Despite her pouring love, talent, and money into his projects, he gave the lead role in his first play, *La Città morta* to Sarah Bernhardt. He later treated Duse so badly before leaving her that both critics and public turned against him. You can't expect to get away with that kind of thing in Italy.

Poet and novelist *Gabriele D'Annunzio* (1863–1938) developed interest in the theater after developing interest in Eleonora Duse in 1896 (they remained in partnership for some years). D'Annunzio took the Greeks, music drama, Wagner, and Nietzsche as his models, but his ambitions for a "total art form" were never

**1865–77** Giuseppe Mengoni designs the Galleria Vittorio Emmanuele in Milan; the shopping arcade, in the form of a cross, is the largest and most elegant of its kind in Europe.

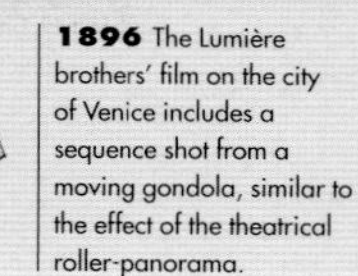

**1896** The Lumière brothers' film on the city of Venice includes a sequence shot from a moving gondola, similar to the effect of the theatrical roller-panorama.

**1900s** Spanish-born theatrical innovator and textile artist Mariano Fortuny creates the effect of a natural sky by playing reflected and diffused colored lights across his revolutionary "cupola" above the stage.

## Supporting Roles

*Of the few writers of merit,* **Giovanni Niccolini** *(1782–1861), whose propagandist* Nabucco *(1819) targeted Napoleon and religious despotism,* **Alessandro Manzoni** *(1785–1873), whose* Il Conte di Carmagnola *(1820) was influenced by Schiller's* Wallenstein, *and* **Paolo Ferrari** *(1822–1873), a comic romantic writer whose* Amore senza Stima *(1868) showed Goldoni's influence, stood out.*

fully realized. *La Città morta* (1898), *La Gioconda* (1898), and *Francesca da Rimini* (1902) all starred Duse.

*Adelaide RISTORI* (1821–1906) was a major actress in Europe and the U.S., playing Lady Macbeth opposite Edwin Booth. Her major rival was the French actress Rachel (stage name of *Elisa FELIX*, 1820–58). *Eleonora DUSE* (1858–1924) was the biggest star. She came from a family of actors (born on a train while on tour, dontcha know), and made her debut at the age of four in *Les Misérables*. She dominated the European stage, rivaling Bernhardt in the U.S., though her spurning of corsets, hair dye, and makeup confused New York socialites. Ristori once called her "the modern woman, with all her maladies of hysteria, anemia, and neurosis."

*Tommaso SALVINI* (1829–1916) was a truly great performer. Also born into a theatrical family, in 1843 he joined a company run by Gustavo Modena, whose tenets of simplicity, naturalness, and psychological truth influenced him. Although Salvini acted in all the major roles, his Othello was considered the most memorable, especially to his Desdemonas, who apparently found his passion in the smothering scene a bit too realistic.

Tommaso Salvini as a notoriously enthusiastic Othello.

**In Character**

In part, Konstantin Stanislavsky's decision to formalize actor training was influenced by watching Tommaso Salvini night after night when he was touring Russia. Stanislavsky observed that Salvini uniquely spent an hour or so before going on stage in preparing himself psychologically. This was revolutionary for its time, since actors normally turned up at the theater just before their character had to be on stage. It's interesting to speculate how he prepared for his well-known Othello. Must have been terrifying for whoever was doing his makeup.

**1857** Björnstjerne Björnson precedes Ibsen as a writer of realistic plays dealing with social problems.

**1895** Bernard Shaw on *Little Eyolf*: "how nicely Mrs. [Patrick] Campbell took the drowning of the child! Just a pretty waving of the fingers, a moderate scream as if she had very nearly walked on a tin tack!"

**1901** The first Nobel prizes are awarded by Alfred Nobel, a successful industrialist who had failed as a novelist and playwright.

1850~1910

# Scandinavian Mysticism

## Ibsen and the Split Personality of Strindberg

Strindberg hallucinating.

*It is said that Henrik* IBSEN *(1828–1906) was a bad-tempered man with few social graces. But so what? Far better that his energies were gainfully employed by an indignant social conscience linked to an enormous talent as a dramatist, than in merely being nice to people.*

In 1866 he wrote a dramatic poem called *Brand*, a searing attack on tightfistedness, pettiness, and compromise. The same anger propelled the writing of the slightly mystic *Peer Gynt* the following year. After this his life and his work became devoted to dramatic realism and left-wing politics, inspired by the social militancy of the Danish critic Georg Brandes. Ibsen's major works, from *A Doll's House* (1879) to *When We Dead Awaken* (1899), placed him as one of Europe's foremost realistic and socially challenging writers and changed the course of world theater. *A Doll's House* promoted female emancipation, *Ghosts* (1881) tackled hereditary syphilis and euthanasia, while *Hedda Gabler* (1890) focused on the individual disaster of women who are not yet ready for emancipation.

If ever a man needed a cold plunge pool, it was *August* STRINDBERG (1849–1912). More versatile than Ibsen, he was much troubled spiritually throughout his life, and his genius was clearly tinged with madness (it's a fine line, dear, a fine line . . .). After teaching, journalism, and library work, his writing entered into a Naturalist phase in the 1880s, when he followed Zola, and then a Symbolist/ Expressionist phase. In the first he wrote

*Peer Gynt* (1994, Royal Shakespeare Co.). Sitting astride a pig and definitely off with the trolls.

**1905** After 91 years of union, Norway becomes independent of Sweden.

**1907** Norway grants its women the right to vote—Britain and the United States will not follow suit until, respectively, 1918 and 1919.

**1908** Painter Edvard Munch, after suffering a mental breakdown, settles permanently in Norway; his best-known painting, *The Scream* (1893), is thought to reflect his childhood trauma.

*The Father* (1887) and *Miss Julie* (1888); the latter's preface is regarded by some as the manifesto for Naturalism. Actually, it's more about Realism—but more of that later! This early work has been accused of violent misogyny, but that is possibly more revealing of those who like to use fashionable psychological labeling than an insight into a highly subjective writer. From 1889 he ran his own experimental theater in Copenhagen, modeled on Antoine's Théâtre-libre. However, the following decade he dropped theater to wrestle with his demons in scientific experiments and occult research. His "Inferno Crisis," a period of five psychotic episodes, put him in a mental hospital and only reading the philosopher Emmanuel Swedenborg saved his mind. The plays that followed, including the "To Damascus" trilogy, *The Dance of Death* (1900), and *A Dream Play* (1902), are his best and show incredible diversity and experimentation.

**PROMPT BOX**

Strindberg, who had "searched for God and found the Devil," was praised by John Synge, the Irish dramatist, who said "Strindberg shakes flame from the living planets and the fixed stars. Ibsen can sit serenely in his Doll's House while Strindberg is battling with heaven and hell." Ibsen himself had remarked about him, "There is one who will be greater than I." Such befitting sanguinity.

## Supporting Roles

*Denmark had* **Adam Oehlenschläger** *(1779–1850), who was a great influence on Ibsen, as was* **Johan Heiberg** *(1791–1860). Then there was* **Hans Christian Andersen** *(1805–75), who considered his plays more important than his fairytales (the world thought otherwise) and* **Hjalmar Bergstrom** *(1868–1914). Denmark being a small country, actors directed, and vice versa, which was nice.*

Henrik Ibsen, 1895, painted by Erik Werenskiold. Note the stern glare of this pillar of society, whose plays scandalized most of his narrow-minded contemporary audiences.

**1824** The Maly (the Russian word for "small") Theater opens, providing a base for a theatrical company formed in 1806; it is the oldest theater in Moscow.

**1832** Tsar Nicholas I commissions the building of the Alexandrinsky Theater in St. Petersburg; he is credited with virtually inventing the patriotic play, encouraging playwrights to flatter him.

**1849** Russian novelist Fyodor Dostoyevsky is sentenced to four years' hard labor in Siberia for political crimes. In *The House of the Dead* (1862), he describes the sadism and squalor of the penal colony.

1800~1900

# Big Plays by Men with Big Facial Hair

## Pushkin, Griboyedov, Gogol, Tolstoy, and Chekhov

*The poet Alexander PUSHKIN (1799-1837) had a large beard and wrote a few good plays. His best was the romantic* Boris Godunov *(1825, produced in 1870), a tragedy about "man's fate and the people's destinies." Nikolai GOGOL (1809–52) was a novelist who wrote one superb farce called* The Government Inspector *(1836), about a town duped by its own paranoia. He merely had a moustache.*

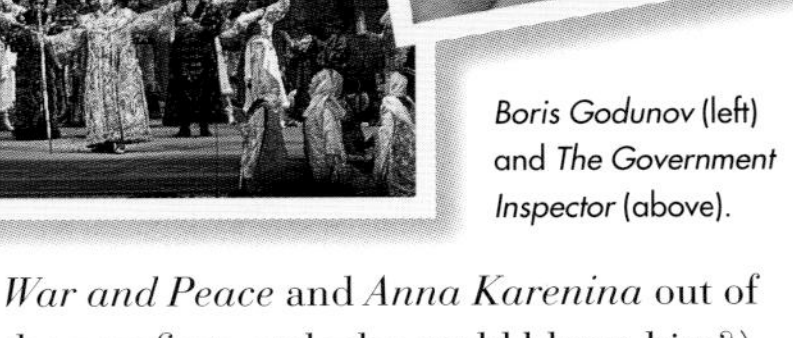

*Boris Godunov* (left) and *The Government Inspector* (above).

*Alexander GRIBOYEDOV* (1795–1829) had a small beard. *His Woe from Wit* (1824), a brilliant philosophical treatise on how a chap gets victimized and imprisoned in a soulless society (you know the feeling), became the basis for Russian national comedy. *Count Leo Nikolayevitch TOLSTOY* (1828–1910) was another novelist, who turned to drama when he was almost 60 (he had to get *War and Peace* and *Anna Karenina* out of the way first, and who could blame him?). His plays were not very good. One of them, *The Light That Shines in Darkness* (1888), concerned a nobleman who wanted to live as Christ but whose wife wouldn't let him ("You're not going into any wilderness, buster, until that drain's unblocked!"). Tolstoy had a huge beard. He ended his days in a shed, having renounced everything except his rampant egomania.

Throughout this century, Russian acting styles, and the role of director, remained traditional and popular. It was left to the best Russian dramatist of them all,

**PROMPT BOX**

Although the Moscow Art Theater takes the spotlight for Russian theaters, there was another theater that had paved the way, as it were. As early as 1853, the Maly Theater in Moscow, which premiered Gogol, Ostrovsky, and Ibsen in Russia, had rejected French Classical and Romantic influence and embraced Realism.

**1858-61** Tzar Alexander II oversees the emancipation of Russian serfs, but they fail to achieve economic independence.

**1891** Construction begins on a Trans-Siberian Railroad to link Moscow with the Pacific coast.

**1899** Prince Volkonsky is appointed director of the Russian Imperial Theaters; attempting to introduce the ideas of designer Alexandre Benois and choreographer Diaghilev, he falls out with both.

*Anton* CHEKHOV (1860–1904), in conjunction with Stanislavsky and the Moscow Art Theater, to bring about a new realistic theater and "naturalistic" acting style. They demanded "natural" responses in actors, so that the inner psychological reactions of their characters to a situation could be more important than the situation itself. Before these men (who both wore neat "goatee" beards) met, Chekhov's plays had been failures, even jeered off the stage because actors and audiences preferred bellowing voices and windmill arm-waving. It is true to say Chekhov's plays, especially *The Seagull* (1896), *Uncle Vanya* (1897), *The Three Sisters* (1901), and *The Cherry Orchard* (1904), created the need for Stanislavsky's acting experiments, and together they changed the face of Russian theater.

So there you have it! Big facial hair = small plays; small facial hair = big plays. (Shakespeare, you'll remember, had a small beard, so that definitively proves the theory.)

## Supporting Roles

**Mikhail Schepkin**, *who had been a serf actor, became known as the father of Realism. His pupils included* **Glikeriya Fedotava** *(who was Stanislavsky's tutor),* **Mariya Ermolova**, **Pavel Mochalov**, *and* **Prov Sadovsky**, *who all helped earn the Maly Theater the title of "the second Moscow University." Schepkin was also responsible during the early part of the century for running the Maly, known as "the house of actors."*

### Training Serfs

Empress Catherine II (the Great) (1762–96) wrote terrible plays but encouraged the theater to be a "national school." Through her the Bolshoi Theater was built in 1771 and an Imperial Theater training school for actors in 1779. She relieved many nobles from state obligations to start a "serf" theater system, where young performers were sponsored (and sometimes beaten) to be great actors.

Looks as though Tolstoy has just singed the end of his beard in a samovar. Painted by Ilya Repin, 1887.

**1878** Mr A. A. Shultz, a hairdresser of Auburn, Massachusetts, discovers that the application of hot towels after shaving makes skin healthier and subsequent shaving easier.

**1885** Benjamin Keith and Edward Albee acquire a chain of vaudeville theaters in major cities across the United States; only with the rise of the movies and radio will vaudeville lose its popularity.

**1890** Thomas Edison advises using 1,000 volts for the first execution by electric chair in New York; the execution is hideously bungled.

1860~1907

# Melodrama, Disaster, and the Follies!

## The U.S. After the Civil War

*By the Civil War, the United States, from east to west, had established a strong mainstream tradition of popular drama. And part of that tradition (derived from European models) was a gloriously moralizing and sentimental style of melodrama.*

The twin evils of drink and slavery were its main concerns. *Uncle Tom's Cabin*, adapted variously from Harriet Beecher Stowe's novel, is a good example, as is *Shenandoah* (1888) by Bronson Howard, which drew inspiration from the Civil War. The main character in *Rip Van Winkle* provided a money-spinning role for the actor Joseph Jefferson. He cocreated the play with one of the best writers of melodramas in the U.S., Irish-born *Dion Boucicault* (1820–1890), who wrote some interesting work, such as *The Colleen Bawn* (1860), *The Octoroon* (1859), and *The Shaughraun* (1874).

**PROMPT BOX**

Melodrama also embraced the Native American as noble hero and the frontiersman (with wonderfully arch names like "Nimrod Wildfire") as an enduring symbol of strength and tenacity associated with the West ("a man's gotta do ..." etc., etc.—you know the sort of thing). Perhaps one of the best known of such heroes was Davy Crockett, who first appeared in 1872 in the melodrama of the same name by Frank Murdoch.

Frank Mayo became associated with the role of Davy Crockett and played it from 1872 till 1896.

Burlesques (e.g., John Brougham's *Pocahontas; or, The Gentle Savage*, 1855) and pantomimes were popular, as were "spectacle" and "disaster" theater with special effects, music, and lavish scenery.

Ever wondered where the idea of tying the heroine to the railroad tracks came from? Well, it was all down to the melodramas of one Augustin Daly; *Under the Gaslight* (1867) had a man tied to the tracks (and rescued by a woman!); a woman was stranded on a ship about to explode in *A Flash of Lightning* (1868),

**1895** Joseph Francis Keaton is nicknamed "Buster" by Harry Houdini when, as a baby, he survives a fall down a flight of stairs without injury.

**1896** Alphonse Mucha's poster for a production of Alfred de Musset's drama *Lorenzaccio* shows French actress Sarah Bernhardt in male attire.

**1906** English engineer George Washington, visiting Guatemala, discovers that coffee boiled at high altitude keeps its flavor—his instant coffee will be included in U.S. army rations.

and a man was strapped to a log as it entered a sawmill in *The Red Scarf* (1868). All in a day's work.

The great American musical took proper shape from about 1840. After European copies, the first truly American musical was *The Black Crook* of 1866, against which ministers fulminated and raged (which they're so good at). Following such wonderful publicity, it ran for 475 performances and established Niblo's Garden as a top venue. Gilbert and Sullivan premiered in 1879 and positioned comic opera as the dominant musical entertainment.

**Behind the Scenes**
Niblo's Garden, which staged *The Black Crook*, was completely redesigned for the occasion. The *Times* reported that the whole stage could be removed, traps introduced anywhere, and entire scenes sunk into the vast cellar. It included music, a melodrama, and a ballet and lasted from 7:45 P.M. to 1:15 A.M. Perhaps that was the real reason why ministers raged against it: it left people too tired to get up in the morning and go to church.

But during the 1890s, changes occurred. Victor Herbert wrote the influential comic opera *Prince Ananias* (1894). Then in 1898 two all-black companies wrote and performed *A Trip to Coontown* and *The Origin of the Cakewalk* (one suspects that the former is unlikely to be revived). As the new century dawned the stage was set for Florenz Ziegfeld's *Follies of 1907*, which shifted the emphasis from humor to elaborate scenery, comedians, and girls, girls, girls!

**A Good Egg**
The greatest exponent of pantomime was George L. Fox, who worked New York's National Theater as a comedian. He produced *Uncle Tom's Cabin* and staged many pantomimes at the Old Bowery theater. An expressive mime, he reached his peak in *Humpty Dumpty* (1868), for 1,200 performances, but in 1875 he went mad on stage and was removed to an asylum. Perhaps someone had pointed out to him that he had played Humpty Dumpty 1,200 times.

Daly's *Under the Gaslight*, where the heroine rescues her lover. The macho movie industry reversed the roles.

**1875** *Swan Lake* is first performed, unsuccessfully, in Moscow, to music by Tchaikovsky; the score is too sophisticated and subtle for musicians and dancers used to "hack" ballet music.

**1897** The S.S. *Turbinia* is the first ship to be driven by a steam turbine.

**1909** American writer and humorist Ring Lardner joins the staff of the *Chicago Tribune* and is assigned to cover the Cubs baseball team.

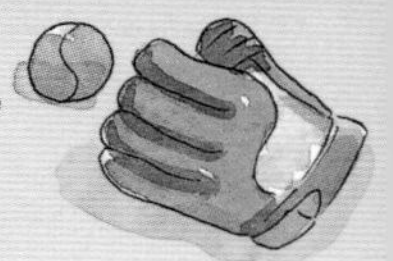

1863~1938

# From Russia with "Loved You, Darling!"

## Stanislavsky: The Father of Acting

*No name in theater has oozed more lovingly from an actor's tongue than that of Konstantin* STANISLAVSKY*—alias Sergeyevich Alekseyev—(1863–1938). The Russian creator of such thespian catchphrases as the "magic if" ("What if this character's situation were real?"), "emotional memory" (using emotive events from one's past to give character motivation—problematic;* *see page 114**), and "you must live the part" (also problematic, e.g., "But Your Honor—I was preparing for the role of Hannibal Lecter!").*

**Danchenko**
Danchenko's role in the Moscow Art Theater has been overshadowed by that of Stanislavsky (mainly because Danchenko wasn't an egotistical actor and didn't write a book called *My Life in Art*, Stanislavsky, 1926). But still it was Danchenko who arranged the historic meeting with Stanislavsky and it was he who lured Chekhov back to theater and revived *The Seagull.*

Although Stanislavsky wasn't the only person to regard acting as a bit more complex than putting on funny hats and pretending to be someone else, he was the first to systematize actor training. He wanted to make it appear "real"—i.e., not acting at all (spot the dilemma). Stanislavsky loathed the semaphore acting, commercial star system, predictable plot, and tacky-backdrop stage design of the bourgeois Russian theater. He wasn't crazy about the typical audience response either (rowdy would be a good word), since he wanted his actors to imagine a "fourth wall" between them and the great unwashed (of course, this wall magically disappeared during applause). Despising mere entertainment, Stanislavsky wanted theater to fulfill a psychologically inspired "cultural mission," to promote those heady realms of education and good citizenry: fun was definitely off the agenda.

**1917** At the end of tsarist rule, Moscow has 16 of the 250 theaters in Russia; 20 years later, it has 60 of the 560 permanent theaters in the Soviet Union.

**1928** Josef Stalin introduces the first Five-Year Plan to collectivize Soviet agriculture; millions of rich peasants are bankrupted or exiled for attempting to resist collectivization.

**1934** Grigori Alexandrov directs the Russian film *Jazz Comedy,* which complies with the official requirement that films should be understood by all.

**PROMPT BOX**

Stanislavsky was aware of, but unable to handle, other new directions in drama. He opened a studio for experimental work, but after inviting Meyerhold to produce Maeterlinck's *The Death of Tintagiles* in 1905, he refused to let the play open because he considered the acting to be "too stylized." So much for experimentation and concern for the audience: if Stan the Man didn't like it, no one else was given a chance to see it.

Stan the Man trying to recapture emotional moments from his past?

In 1897, he had an 18-hour conversation with playwright *Vladimir Nemirovich-Danchenko* (1858–1943)—I timed it myself—and they decided to collaborate in founding the Moscow Art Theater. The following year saw his great artistic partnership with playwright Anton Chekhov producing/directing *The Seagull* (1898), *Uncle Vanya* (1899), *The Three Sisters* (1901), and *The Cherry Orchard* (1904). It was struggling with the new "untheatrical realism" of Chekhov's work, as well as with other avant-garde theater developments (e.g., Symbolism), the failure of his Studio under Meyerhold (see page 108), and finally "sitting on a bench in Finland and examining my artistic past" (1906) that spurred Stanislavsky to formalize a whole new approach to acting. This "System," as it became known, was to be the most dominant influence in 20th-century Western theater performance.

**Behind the Scenes**

The realistic box sets with their "imaginary fourth wall" (an idea from Antoine's experiments with the Théâtre-libre) made few compromises to sightlines and visibility. And, although the Moscow Art Theater used real furniture, props, food, and so forth, they also made wide use of painted backdrops and sometimes even two-dimensional painted trees. Well . . . even big, burly, butch Russian stagehands didn't feel like lugging trees on and off stage. And I for one wouldn't argue with *them*.

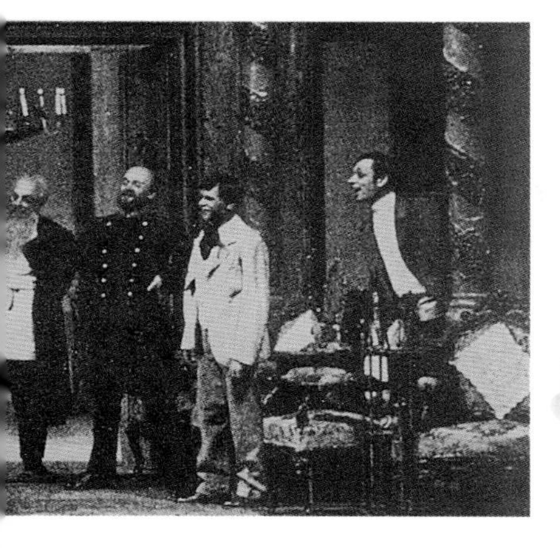

The original 1904 MAT production of *The Cherry Orchard.*

**1892** Belgian architect Baron Victor Horta designs his first major work, Tassel House in Brussels; the Art Nouveau interior displays his characteristic whiplash lines on wall decorations, doors, and staircases.

**1893** French Jews are blamed for the collapse of the Panama Canal Co., whose bankruptcy has cost many French investors their savings.

**1900** The *Guide Michelin*, financed by tire-manufacturers André and Édouard Michelin, is published in Paris, the first systematic evaluation of European restaurants.

1890~1920

# Mysticism, Romance, and Symbolism

## The French and the Russians

Symbolism!

*As Realism swept the West, many felt there was a bit more to theater than boring representations of some idiot's view of "reality." In the last decade of the 19th century, a movement calling itself "Symbolism" emerged from France (known for its Big Movements—ask any doctor) to return drama once again to its symbolical and mythical roots.*

Taking Wagner and Nietzsche as mentors, subjective Symbolism placed the individual/artist as hero in his own life, in a mystical drama that revealed inner states and where mood and evocation replaced bald statement and linear narrative. Stage managers liked it too; they didn't have to worry about "authentic" props. But then again, they did have to find "authentic" audiences.

In 1890 the 18-year-old Paul Fort opened the Théâtre d'Art in Paris, committing it to Symbolism with a production of *The Intruder* (1890) by the Belgian writer *Maurice MAETERLINCK* (1862–1949). The Antoine-trained actor *Aurelian LUGNÉ-POE* (1869–1940) took over the Théâtre d'Art in 1893 and renamed it the Théâtre l'Oeuvre. Fort's house style was stylized/abstract décor, unrealistic intoned dialogue, and a dream-like atmosphere, which perfectly suited Maeterlinck's mystical dramas. Acting was also stylized because Maeterlinck originally wrote characters for marionettes (he didn't think much of actors—an attitude shared by other practitioners, e.g., Jarry, Craig). Fort also produced *Ubu Roi* by Alfred Jarry in 1896 for just two performances (although he regretted that; see page 106). Not all was radical experiment. In 1897, *Edmond ROSTAND* (1868–1918) saw his

The eloquent Cyrano (he's the one on the right).

**1912** Belgian painter and sculptor Rik Wouters completes his bronze *The Mad Virgin*, inspired by American-born dancer Isadora Duncan.

**1913** American manufacturer Henry Ford introduces assembly-line production, increasing efficiency and reducing costs to make cheaper cars.

**1920** Agatha Christie's fictional Belgian detective Hercule Poirot makes his first appearance in *The Mysterious Affair at Styles*.

A drawing of the 1920 staging for Evreinov's *The Storming of the Winter Palace*. This was BIG theater worthy of a BIG revolution.

**PROMPT BOX**

Apart from writing *The Inspector General* (1912), which parodied various directors' approaches to Gogol's play, and *The Fourth Wall* (1915), which revealed the stupidity of Stanislavsky's devices in relation to opera (or perhaps the stupidity of opera in relation to Stanislavsky's devices?), Evreinov's greatest achievement was scripting and staging *The Storming of the Winter Palace* (1920), with a cast of 10,000 on Uritsky Square in St. Petersburg. Everybody works!

work about the poet with the big nose, *Cyrano de Bergerac*, produced.

In Russia the Symbolist poet and dramatist *Alexandr Blok* (1880–1921) was influenced by popular theater forms and the mysticism of the philosopher Vladimir Solovyov (as were many other young writers, including Bely; see box, right). Blok wrote *The Puppet Play* (1906), rewriting "commedia" characters as God-seekers and apocalyptic seers (Go for it, Al!). But perhaps the most complete antirealistic man of the theater was *Nikolai Evreinov* (1879–1953). Although not a great writer, he was immensely original. A dramatist-director-theorist and historian, he tried to revitalize theater by rediscovering it as imaginative play (which preceded arguments about literary value and aesthetics). He wrote *An Introduction to Monodrama* (1909), which sought to define the audience as co-creator and help dissolve the boundary between theater and life.

### Supporting Roles

*The first half of* **Alexandr Blok***'s life embraced Symbolism and mysticism, the second half a staunch Realism. What caused this change of heart? Partly the failure of the 1905 Revolution, which upset Blok spiritually, but also perhaps the fact that his wife had a glad eye for* **Andrei Bely**, *his Symbolist colleague. Blok later called Symbolists "decadent charlatans." I wonder why?*

**1920** Adolph Levitt founds the Donut Corporation, which markets a doughnut-making machine and ready-prepared mix.

**1922** When 40,000 black-shirted Italian Fascists demand strong government, King Victor Emmanuel appoints former schoolmaster and journalist Benito Mussolini, Il Duce, to the post of prime minister.

**1924** Bronislava Nijinska's ballet *Les Biches*, with music by Poulenc, is performed for the first time by the Ballets Russes in Monte Carlo.

1920~1940

# Illogical and Unreal, but So Happy

## The Futurists

*Given the overwhelming changes visited upon the Western world from the last decade of the 19th century to the end of World War I (including cars, planes, electricity, mass production, psychoanalysis, etc.), it's hardly surprising that art, always in the vanguard of social change, should wrestle with the enormous implications.*

### Supporting Roles

**Bruno Corra** *(1892–1976) and* **Emilio Settimelli** *(1891–1954) wrote sketches and plays for live performance. They also contributed to the* Manifesto of Futurist Cinema *in 1916. Futurists were great supporters of film, even making their own (Settimelli appears in one,* Vita Futurista*). In 1910, Corra was the first to paint directly onto film, a technique copied and developed by later artists.*

*These mostly came from wealthy Italian families who didn't know that paper is actually cheaper.*

Marinetti (known in his time as "the Caffeine of Europe") in a pose suggesting either a certain confidence or starchy trousers.

In *Le Figaro* in February 1909, *Filippo T. Marinetti* (1876–1944) wrote an article entitled "The Founding and Manifesto of Futurism," following it in 1915 with "From the Futurist Synthetic Theater." In both he called for art to embrace new technology and the spontaneity, dynamism, speed, and movement of the machine. "Get rid of the past," he cried, "including all its art galleries, museums, academics, concert halls, 'prose' and 'musical' theater, and especially realism and naturalism," because "It's stupid to

**1934** Italy defeats Czechoslovakia at Rome's Stadio Torino, winning the World Cup soccer competition.

**1939** American poet Ezra Pound begins making pro-Fascist broadcasts from Rome to the United States.

**1940** Leon Trotsky, a prime mover of the Russian Revolution, dies in a hospital in Mexico City; he has been struck on the head with an icepick by Ramon Mercader, possibly an agent of Stalin.

**PROMPT BOX**

Futurism is often associated with Italian Fascism, especially during its "second" phase. But this connection is spurious, since, as explained above, Russian Futurists embraced the diametrically opposed Communist revolution with as much enthusiasm. Marinetti himself, however, was a friend of Mussolini and a great supporter of Fascism. More importantly, Futurism is inherently fascistic in its violent insistence on disregarding everything except its own references.

write a hundred pages when one will do!" and, "IT'S STUPID TO RENOUNCE THE DYNAMIC LEAP IN THE VOID OF TOTAL CREATION!" Perhaps I'd better throw those mushrooms away.

Marinetti wanted instead an "illogical," "unreal" theater with poems, readings, paintings, sculptures, and performance "works" all being performed and created simultaneously. The intention was to provoke outrage, which would shake the audience out of its cozy apathy. Enrico Prampolini, a later Futurist, called for a new staging, a "colorless electromechanical architecture" lit by electricity and colored glass, machines to produce abstractions, and an actor who was reduced to a robotlike function. The Futurists set up about 500 of their "syntheses" (compressed dramatic examples of Futurist theater), but hardly any were performed. A second phase of the group's activities came in the 1930s, but by then it had become even more weak and amateurish and was little more than a posing avant-garde.

News of their activities extended to Russia, where the brilliant *Vladimir Mayakovsky* (1893–1930) proclaimed himself a Futurist and the "loud-mouthed Zoroaster" of his age. His plays, including *Vladimir Mayakovsky, A Tragedy* (1913) and *Mystery-Bouffe* (1918), embody his preoccupations with time and its effects on personality (his own). His major works, *The Bedbug* (1929) and *The Bath-House* (1930), were grotesque satires sharply criticizing the Communist bureaucracy and parodying the future Soviet utopia. It is thought that their lukewarm reception contributed to his suicide.

Mayakovsy looking as though he's just read the reviews of *The Bedbug*.

**Behind the Scenes**

Many a director has shrieked "Get Rid of Those Actors!" But Enrico Prampolini, second-generation Futurist and innovative theater designer, director, painter, and sculptor, tried to dispense with them permanently. In the *Machine Art Manifesto* (1923), he argued that properly built mechanical scenery with elevators, lighting, phonograph recordings, etc., would do a far better job than any bunch of actors. Years later his dream would come true with many of London's West End hit musicals taking the stage.

**1850** *La Dame aux camélias* by Alexandre Dumas *fils* is performed for the first time; the play is an early example of French social drama.

**1872–73** Monsieur Marcel, *le roi de l'ondulation*, invents the Marcel Wave; ten years later, he can afford to retire.

**1902** Vsevolod Meyerhold founds the Society of New Drama in Russia; he eliminates scenery and treats the actor as a puppet in the hands of the director.

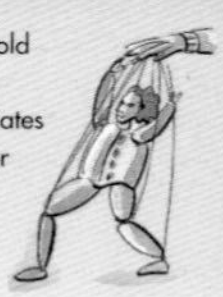

1850~1922

# Take Your Pick. We Got Naturalism...

## Hauptmann, Gorky, O'Neill

*Since Tom Robertson put real bread and tea on stage in 1860 (see pages 74–5), academics have got their knickers in a twist (normal dress code for many of them) in defining "Naturalism" and "Realism" and what, exactly, is the difference between them.*

Maksim Gorky photographed in 1900, looking down but not out.

Although, in both, action arises from character, logic from sentiments, and plot from plain old life (working-class was de rigeur), Realism is a style, a "real-seemingness," in a performance where, despite the apparent reality of the proceedings, it is no more "real" than any other artistic form you may care to mention. Naturalism is much the same except it is claimed there is a greater depth to the relationship between character and environment (which is usually one of utter misery). Raymond Williams, in *English Drama: Forms and Development* (1977), said "Naturalistic" characters' lives "soaked into their environment ... and the environment ... soaked into the lives." There you are; is that all clear now?

**Behind the Scenes**
Naturalism has made thespians do the silliest things to maintain the illusion of the "fourth wall": actors facing the audience and "warming" their hands at an invisible fire; or the mirror on the back wall painted to look like it 's reflecting wallpaper and not the audience. It was a sad day when audiences stopped throwing things at the stage, considering what some actors chuck at audiences.

Anyway, Naturalism plugged the gap created by the general 19th-century subject matter of the "classical" stage and "real" lives of ordinary people. In Germany, *Gerhart* HAUPTMANN (1862–1946) wrote *The Weavers* (1892), a major Naturalist drama of "the workers," where the

**1902** French novelist and polemicist Émile Zola dies of asphyxiation from carbon monoxide fumes due to a blocked chimney.

**1908** The First International Congress of Psychoanalysis is held in Salzburg; Freud, Brill, Adler, and Jung attend.

**1919** In protest against the Treaty of Versailles, Rear-Admiral von Reuter orders seamen to scuttle the entire German fleet in the harbor at Scapa Flow in the Orkney Islands.

Laurence Olivier and Dorothy Cummings in *Long Day's Journey into Night* at London's National Theater.

## Supporting Roles

*Among other "classics" of Naturalism are* The Happy Family *(1890), a German play by* **Arno Holz** *and* **Johannes Schlaf** *about a family that was anything but, and the boring English mining plays of D. H. Lawrence. Today, television soap operas are Naturalism par excellence, and it seems that some poor souls even send birthday presents to fictional characters. Proof, I think, that the human race is doomed.*

crowd is the hero. In Russia, *Maksim GORKY* (*Alexei PESHKOV*, 1868–1936) wrote *The Lower Depths* (1902), an angry and sympathetic view of down-and-outs. Gorky was not a happy man in any event; even his *nom de plume* meant "Maksim the Bitter." In the U.S., *Eugene O'NEILL* (1888–1953), who claimed Strindberg as his mentor, tried living in the "lower depths" for a while. His best contributions to Naturalism were his "sea plays," *Bound East for Cardiff*, *In the Zone*, *The Long Voyage Home*, and the *Moon of the Caribbees* (all 1914–19), although he wrote in several genres.

The main problem with Naturalism is that of compromising the artifice of theater, which is at its heart. Novelty devices like real tea, food, grass (yes, I've actually had hay fever in a theater), etc., reduce theater's primary source of power, the imagination. Additionally, Naturalism has meant that stage design has been governed not by creative expression, but by a 20th-century obsession with "authenticity."

Eugene O'Neill and Agnes Boulton on the verandah of their house in Massachusetts.

**1856** French novelist Gustave Flaubert's *Madame Bovary* is declared an immoral novel; both he and his publisher are prosecuted.

**1889** Painter Carl Larsson returns from Paris to Sweden; his paintings of idealized everyday life, using clear, transparent colors, will influence interior design.

**1901** In reprisal for his repression of student agitators, the Russian propaganda minister is assassinated.

1850~1950

# ... Or We Got Realism

## Europe and the States

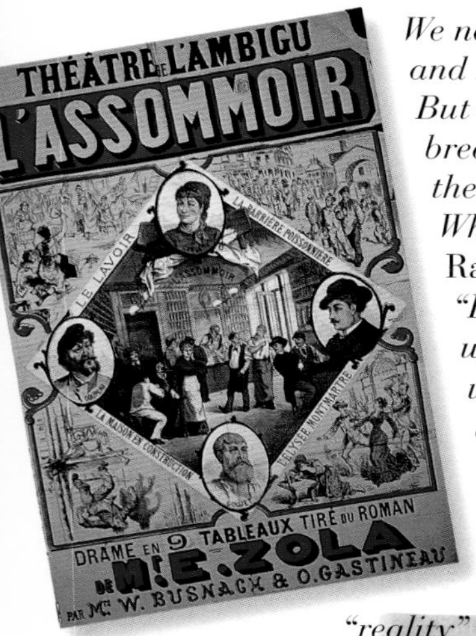


Zola's *L'Assommoir* (1877) is set in the taverns of Paris.

*We now understand that "Realism" is itself a style and no closer to reality than any other art form. But in 19th-century Europe it represented a breakthrough in displacing the Romantic theater, which had become very predictable. When Émile Zola dramatized his novel* Thérèse Raquin *in 1873 (probably the first truly "Realist" play), it was claimed that theater was finally representing the "reality" of unheroic ordinary lives on stage. But Zola's drama was very dull and literal in its slavish adherence to all things "natural." It was left to later writers, like Ibsen, Strindberg, and Chekhov, to show what the theater really needed—not "reality" but the impression of reality. Realism not only redefined the structure and style of a production, but also consolidated something else: just as an orchestra needs the conductor, theater now found that it needed the director.*

I have already mentioned European "Realist" directors such as Saxe-Meinengen, Antoine, Stanislavsky, etc., because that is where the impulse began. But by the end of the century Realism was also entering the American mainstream alongside vaudeville,

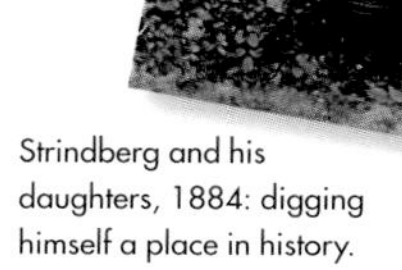

Strindberg and his daughters, 1884: digging himself a place in history.

melodrama, and the spectacular. *David Belasco* (1853–1931), a writer of (forgettable) realistic plays, is best remembered for the pioneering and meticulous realism of his essentially melodramatic productions (even transferring real buildings to the stage). The designer *Norman Bel Geddes* (1893–1958) was probably most famous for being the "father of streamlining" in industrial design and some brilliant Symbolist theater designs (e.g., *The Miracle*, 1923). But he also designed very realistic sets, including *Dead End* (1935).

**Behind the Scenes**
When Stanislavsky staged Andreyev's *The Life of Man*, he covered the stage in black velvet and put on it "sets" of rope, a different color for each act. Actors also wore black costumes with rope outlines. Although it was successful, Stan was unhappy. "I do not feel the actors have moved forward," he said. Perhaps they couldn't see, Stan.

Taking the Moscow Art Theater as their model, in 1931 a group of artists including Lee Strasberg (who formulated Method acting—see page 114), Harold Clurman, and Cheryl Crawford began an experiment called the Group Theater as a platform for new American plays of social significance. Actually they engendered more good actors (e.g., John Garfield, Morris Carnovsky, Franchot Tone) than writers, although one, the brilliant and Chekhovian *Clifford Odets* (1906–63), gave the Group its voice as he transformed working-class life into poetry with works such as *Waiting for Lefty*, *Awake and Sing!*, and *Paradise Lost*, all premiering in 1935.

Peter Gowen and Janet McTeer in a scene from Ibsen's *A Doll's House*. No doubt the letter contained some "real" words.

**PROMPT BOX**

Realism is the dominant mode of dramatic representation in film and television. Film is able to use other forms, such as Expressionism, Surrealism, and, of course, spectacle. Television mostly uses Realism or Naturalism, with occasional tame forays into other forms (e.g., game shows and the like).

**Suffering for Art**
To challenge his actors performing in a production of Hauptmann's *The Sunken Bell*, Stanislavsky dangerously broke up the surface of the stage. "Let them creep . . . (and) sit on stones. Let them descend into the trap and climb out again," he said. This would "force them to get used to a new mise-en-scène." Today's actors would respond: "Let me phone my union, my lawyer . . ."

**1907** Australian swimmer Annette Hellerman is arrested on a Boston beach for wearing a one-piece swimsuit without a skirt.

**1914** John Singer Sargent's portrait of Henry James is mutilated by a suffragette on the first day of its exhibition in London.

**1916** Eugene O'Neill's *Before Breakfast* is staged in Greenwich Village; the author plays a character whose only utterance is a gurgle as he slashes his throat with a razor.

1907~1925

# Or If It's Been a Bad Hair Day...

## How About Expressionism?

*Expressionism as a concept sprang from painting, and has been used to mean every kind of nonrealism imaginable, including Surrealism. Unlike Realism, which represents how external "reality" affects the artist, "Expressionism" describes how an artist imposes his own concept of reality on the outside world by expressing his own emotional experience (which is fine unless the artist is barking mad). Or something like that.*

### *Supporting Roles*

The Son *(1917), by* **Walter Hasenclever** *(1890–1940), was a key Expressionist work;* Heaven and Earth *(1920), by* **Paul Kornfeld** *(1889–1942), marked a high point for Expressionist theater. Originally a "Naturalist,"* **Leopold Jessner** *(1878–1945) turned Shakespeare's* Richard III *into an Expressionist play. There were also* **Reinhard Sorge** *(1892–1916), a so-called ecstatic Expressionist,* **Reinhard Goering** *(1887–1936),* **Arnolt Bronnen** *(1895–1959), and* **Otto Falckenberg** *(1873–1947).*

Like all movements, Expressionism has its forerunners, in this case Strindberg and *Frank WEDEKIND* (1864–1918). Wedekind's plays departed from Naturalism in their episodic structure and grotesque caricatures as characters. His first major work, *Spring's Awakening* (1901), did not get performed until 1906 because of its radical form and shocking theme (adolescent sex. Quite right too! Everyone knows girls and boys don't do it

Toller wrote *The Machine Wreckers* while in prison for advocating Communism.

**1920** The Bloody Mary cocktail is invented by a bartender at Harry's New York Bar in Paris.

**1923** Maidenform brassières are introduced to give girls a bit of an uplift.

**1924** Adolf Hitler is convicted of high treason and sentenced to five years in prison, where he starts writing *Mein Kampf* (*My Struggle*).

Oskar Kokoschka checking that there's nothing Expressionist up his sleeve.

until they're 21!). The "Lulu" plays, *Earth Spirit* (1895) and *Pandora's Box* (1904), also depict a society obsessed by lust and greed. So what else is new?

*Oskar* KOKOSCHKA (1886–1980), apart from having a name that sounds like someone sneezing, was a highly influential painter and dramatist who provided some of the earliest examples of Expressionism. His *Sphinx and Strawman* (1907) was one of the most impressive theatrical excursions into the subconscious and influenced the later Dadaist theater (see page 106). Two names most associated with German Expressionism are *Ernst* TOLLER (1893–1939) and *Georg* KAISER (1878–1945). Toller's *Masses and Man* (1920) and *The Machine Wreckers* (1922) depict strike action and Luddite attacks on factories by worker/slaves. Kaiser, in *From Morn to Midnight* (1917), created a modern Morality play, which took a lowly clerk on a distorted, dreamlike, and episodic journey for spiritual enlightenment. Expressionist theater traveled to the U.S., where Eugene O'Neill (see page 95) wrote two great Expressionist plays, *The Emperor Jones* (1920) and *The Hairy Ape* (1921), which caused the critic John Willett to call him the best Expressionist dramatist of all.

Britain, as always, wasn't tolerating any damn silly foreign ideas, so anyone attempting to import one had to leave it at Passport Control and pick it up on the way out. And the sooner the better!

**Cabaret**

Frank Wedekind sang rude ditties in the infamous "Die elf Scharfrichter" ("The Eleven Executioners") club in Munich. Cabaret was then a popular entertainment across Europe. Clubs called "Black Cat" (Paris), "Noise and Smoke" (Munich), "Four Cats" (Barcelona), and "The Bat" (Moscow) all served a "menu" of salacious poems, music, and sketches. It is rumored that Wedekind was once ejected for urinating on the audience. They didn't find it too funny, strangely enough.

**PROMPT BOX**

Ernst Toller was a passionately political man who founded a militant-pacifist group. He became president of the first short-lived Bavarian Soviet Republic in 1918 and later commander of its Red Army. Then he spent five years in prison when the "Republic" fell in 1919. He committed suicide as World War II broke out.

**1892** The first lavatories are provided on British trains; hitherto, ladies traveling on long journeys (in segregated carriages) have had to bring their own chamber pots.

**1902** British novelist and essayist Samuel Butler dies; at his own request, his ashes are buried anonymously in the crematorium garden.

**1905** The New York production of George Bernard Shaw's *Mrs. Warren's Profession* is closed by the police because it is an "immoral" play; the first London production is in 1926.

1890~1915

# Jewels in the Dross

## Irony and Fantasy in England

*While Europe and the United States were having so much fun with Expressionism and cabaret, etc., what were English thesps up to? Being dull and pompous, that's what. In late Victorian and Edwardian England most "serious" theatrical output was dire and, like everything else in that era, obsessively snobbish and class-divisive.*

Poster showing G. B. Shaw as a Russian demon king.

Poster for Harley Granville-Barker's production of *The Taming of the Shrew* at the Royal Court Theater.

Music hall (constantly under attack from a puffed-up self-righteous middle class), despite odd flashes of genius, all too often descended into self-parody, while melodrama, the regular fare of the theaters, was mawkishly sentimental and moralizing. Spectacular shows blossomed at the Hippodrome and Coliseum, but they were little more than novelties produced by men who would do anything to make money (rather like those in the West End and Broadway over the last 30 years).

However, a few rose above the dross, and they mainly came from Ireland. Actor, playwright, director, and critic *Harley Granville-Barker* (1877–1946), a major influence on British theater, took over the Royal Court in 1904 and bravely initiated new work, including 11 plays by *George Bernard Shaw* (1856–1950) (this was brave in itself!). The Irish-born Shaw wrote endlessly and influentially about everything. His plays, trademarked by ironic and witty iconoclasm, were often confrontational—such as *Widowers' Houses* (1892), about slum landlords, and *Mrs. Warren's Profession* (1902), about prostitution. The later *John Bull's Other*

**1909** Robert E. Peary claims to be the first person to reach the North Pole; later research suggests he got his sums wrong and was actually between 30 and 60 miles away.

**1910** The first exhibition of post-impressionists is held at London's Grafton Gallery, with work by van Gogh, Cézanne, and Matisse.

**1914** German and British soldiers declare a truce on Christmas day; they play soccer and exchange gifts before resuming hostilities the next day.

## *Supporting Roles*

*The melodramas of* **Henry Jones** *(1851–1929), such as* Saints and Sinners *(1884) and* The Case of Rebellious Susan *(1894), although successful, revealed a timidity in criticizing the stifling contemporary moral values.* **Arthur Wing Pinero** *(1855–1934) also chose not to stick his neck out too far.* The Second Mrs. Tanqueray *(1893) ends obsequiously when his heroine commits suicide just because she doesn't fit in.*

*Island* (1904) was Shaw's first successful play in London; it grappled with that vexing "Irish question," which, as we all know, is still being grappled with now.

*Oscar Wilde* (1854–1900), also an Irishman, had more drama in his life than his plays. His intention was to satirize, ruthlessly, the dull and pompous melodrama that was the order of the day, but nevertheless, even his best work, *The Importance of Being Ernest* (1895), was, like all his plays, drama, not theater. That is, though witty and socially pertinent, the plot contrivances are weak and the staging unadventurous. Publicity about Wilde's homosexuality, and the court trials that followed, closed the play and put him in prison. He was declared bankrupt, spent his last years wandering around Europe, and died in Paris.

Other names to note include the novelist *John Galsworthy* (1867–1933), who wrote *The Silver Box* (1906), *Strife* (1909), and *Justice* (1910), all produced by Granville-Barker and dealing with social and moral themes. *J. M. Barrie* (1860–1937), author of *Peter Pan* (1904), *The Admirable Crichton* (1902), and *Quality Street* (1902), injected a note of well-crafted escapist fantasy (if a little overromantic and whimsical) into otherwise social dramas.

An 1884 Oscar Wilde caricature captures the contemptuous expression.

**Behind the Scenes**

The Hippodrome (built in 1900 as a circus) had a large water tank for aquatic spectacles (no, not swimming goggles). In 1910 it premiered Tchaikovsky's *Swan Lake* (literally!). The Coliseum (1904) was the first music hall in England to possess a revolving stage. A venue for Diaghilev's Ballets Russes and ice shows, in 1968 it became the home of the English National Opera.

Water ballet at the Hippodrome.

**1900** John Millington Synge, working as a literary critic in Paris, makes a third trip to the Aran Islands; W. B. Yeats has advised him to go there and "express a life that has never found expression."

**1901** James Joyce, an undergraduate at Dublin University, attacks the proposed National Theater for Ireland in a two-penny pamphlet called "The Day of Rabblement."

**1917** Mata Hari, an exotic dancer known for her scanty costumes and love of feathers, is executed as a spy.

1899~1940

# Of Playboys and Gunmen

## The Irish Connection

J. M. Synge, painted by Jack Butler Yeats. Behind those calm, steady eyes, an angry man fumed at the church and the English state.

*It takes more than 300 years of English repression of Gaelic culture to stop the Irish from being a very literary and poetic people (as the customers of any Irish pub will tell you—endlessly). So it's no surprise that in 1897, W. B. YEATS (1865–1939), along with Lady Augusta GREGORY (1852–1932), formed the "Irish Literary Society" in Dublin to help de-Anglicize the arts and effectively start a long-overdue Irish national theater.*

Inspired by Lady Gregory's translations of Irish heroic legends, Yeats wrote romantic heroic verse dramas like *The Countess Cathleen* (1899). He joined forces with the amateur Irish National Dramatic Society, which had produced *The Shadow of the Glen* by the then unknown Irish writer J. M. Synge, to become the Irish National Theater Society in 1904, which then became the Abbey Theater (later giving none other than Orson Welles his first acting job). *J[ohn] M[illington] SYNGE* (1871–1909) had lived in Paris and the Aran Islands. This gave him material for his best work, *Riders to the Sea* (1904), *The Tinker's Wedding* (its

**Annie Horniman**

Ironically the profits of English colonialism financed the Irish National Theater. In 1894 Annie Horniman inherited her father's tea fortune and began financing the activities of Yeats's enterprise, including the Abbey Theater (1904). In 1907 disagreements forced her to leave. She then set up the very first English repertory company in Manchester. They had their opening season at the Midland Hotel Theater.

**1918** The "Shingle" style of short hair for women will be followed in 1931 by the Mingle and the Cringle.

**1926** When the audience riots at a performance of Sean O'Casey's *The Plough and the Stars* at the Abbey Theater in Dublin, W. B. Yeats tells them, "You have disgraced yourselves again."

**1939** Dublin-born poet, dramatist, and Senator of the Irish Free State, W. B. Yeats dies and is buried in France; after the war, his body is transferred to the Drumcliffe Churchyard in County Sligo.

anticlerical tone so frightened the Abbey, let alone the church, it wasn't produced until 1971), and most famously *The Playboy of the Western World*, which caused riots in 1907. Although he used realistic sets and props, he elevated peasant speech to dramatic poetic rhetoric. His settings might be workers' cottages, but his characters were wild and fantastic, like Christy, an outcast artist "Playboy" with attitude.

Yeats and the Abbey stuck with the proscenium arch and box set until the 1950s, letting the language dominate the work. This is especially true of plays by *Sean O'CASEY* (1880–1964). At first his political themes were realistically set, as in *The Shadow of a Gunman* (1923), which dealt with the Anglo-Irish war before the 1921 settlement; *Juno and the Paycock* (1924), set after the settlement during the Civil War; and *The Plough and the Stars* (1926), a version of the 1916 uprising. But he experimented, and when he offered *The Silver Tassie* (1928), which included Expressionist ideas, the Abbey refused it. O'Casey was outraged, broke contact with the company, and departed for England.

### *Supporting Roles*

**Padraic Colum** *(1881–1972), member of the Irish National Theater Society, wrote* Broken Soil *(1903) and* The Land *(1905).* **William Boyle** *(1853–1923) with* The Building Fund *(1905), and* **T. C. Murray** *(1873–1959) in* Birthright *(1910), continued the tradition of Realist Irish writers. The brilliant fantasy plays of* **George Fitzmaurice** *(1877–1963), like* The Pie-Dish *(1908), marked a welcome exception.*

**PROMPT BOX**

Synge's comedy *The Playboy of the Western World*, which somewhat challenged the unquestionable purity of Irish morals, upset more than a self-righteous Dublin audience. On its opening night in New York in 1911, Irish-Americans also rioted. But ex-President Theodore Roosevelt, who attended the opening, gave a glowing appraisal of both play and players to the press, which silenced most opposition.

An unholy Irish row erupts in O'Casey's *The Plough and the Stars.*

**1871** Over 19 percent of men and 26 percent of women in Britain cannot sign the parish register when they marry; by 1891, the percentage will drop to about 7 percent.

**1881** The Duke of Saxe-Meinengen's Meinengen Players perform at Drury Lane Theater in London; the use of split-staging, crowd choreography, and the conception of a production as a whole are revolutionary.

**1895** The first game of professional football is played in the United States.

1849~1935

# A Shutter in the Dark

## Craig, Appia, Wagner, Constructivism

*Two of the most influential "visionaries" in Western theater were the Englishman (Edward) Gordon* CRAIG *(1872–1966) and the Swiss Adolphe* APPIA *(1862–1928). In* The Art of the Theater *(1905), Craig called for a nonnaturalistic "director's" theater that would appeal to the emotions through movement alone.*

Gordon Craig's 1928 set for *Macbeth* must have made the actors somewhat nervous.

He was full of plans to sweep away boring realism and the dominance of "words," but, like those of most visionaries, his ideas couldn't be built. His 98-foot-high shutters, to be moved by "invisible" means, or his fluid architectural shapes, to be created during a performance, were parts of what he called "scene"; everyone else called them "impossible." (One wonders if he developed theories as to the breeding of a superhuman stage crew.)

### Collapsing Hamlet

Stanislavsky invited Craig to design and direct *Hamlet* in 1912. Craig wanted huge screens built out of metal. Stanislavsky said that was too heavy, so Craig suggested the Moscow Art Theater be rebuilt! They compromised on canvas and wood (giving us our modern "flats"). After two years of preparation the play opened, but two hours before curtain up, the whole edifice collapsed.

Appia emphasized the power of focused electric light (still in its infancy) to "color" moods and create mystery or symbolism. By writing "scores" for lights, just as choreographers did for dance, he gave the world the lighting "plot" (which in turn unfortunately gave us that bizarre sub-species, the lighting technician). Nowadays he could probably have gotten a job working for Pink Floyd.

### PROMPT BOX

Craig wanted to do away with the actor (which one he didn't say). "The actor is for me only an insuperable difficulty and expense," he said. He declared that an "Übermarionette," or super puppet, totally manipulated by the "puppeteer" (the director, of course) would be the best actor. I think there are a few out there now, Gordon.

**1903** Researchers working for German coffee importer Ludwig Roselius invent a process to remove caffeine from the beans; the result is Sanka (sans caffeine).

**1907** American novelist Theodore Dreiser becomes editor of *Butterick Publications;* he manages to slip in poems between the dress patterns and advice to the Jenny Wren Club.

**1927** American dancer and sometime lover of Edward Gordon Craig, Isadora Duncan dies in a racing car, strangled by her long scarf.

The gate for such ideas had been opened by the *Gesamtkunstwerk*, or "total artwork" idea of Richard Wagner (see page 77) based on the (then radical) notion that all elements in a production should be unified. Wagner had a theater built at Bayreuth in 1876 to demonstrate his theory (those were the days!). *Gesamtkunstwerk* would, he claimed, provide a "communal experience" for performers and audience.

## *Supporting Roles*

**Max Reinhardt** *(1873–1943), one of the first directors (after Saxe-Meinengen), became famous for encouraging new acting techniques and scenic design (he used the revolving stage—an idea originally stolen from the Japanese), although his productions were always illusionistic. Most associated with the Deutsches Theater, Berlin (until the Nazis arrived), he later worked in Salzburg, Vienna, and the United States.*

However, another of Wagner's bright ideas, the darkening of the auditorium during the performance, changed all future theater beyond recognition. From that moment, the fundamental sense of unity and social interaction between audience and players, essential to theater from the earliest rituals, was gone. Audiences were psychologically "shut out" from events on stage; they became voyeurs. (Let's face it, sitting in the dark watching others is in any circumstances a questionable thing to do!) So much for a "communal experience"!

**Behind the Scenes**

Wagner's Bayreuth theater (1876) dispensed with things like boxes, pit, galleries, etc., in favor of "democratic" seating such as we are now used to. The auditorium contained 30 rows of seats, which were arranged in a fan shape, doubling in width from front to back, and with aisles on either side instead of in the center.

In Russia, Lyubov Popova, Vladimir Tatlin, and others declared "Constructivism" as the design aesthetic of the machine age. Like the Expressionists and Futurists, they saw design as a combination of abstract vision and the laws of mechanics. Vsevolod Meyerhold, the brilliant director, utilized Constructivist theory for both actor training and staging (see page 108).

For the production of Wagner's *Walküre* in Paris in 1893, they used lights and a cyclorama screen to make the horse-riding scenes realistic.

**1896** In Germany, Karl Lautenschlüger introduces the first revolving stage.

**1903** Arthur Conan Doyle agrees to bring Sherlock Holmes back from the dead and is paid $5,000 each for at least six stories.

**1904** Charles Rolls and Henry Royce become partners in a new car-making business.

1896~1930

# Mad People and Modernists

## From Dada to Ubu

*Perhaps the craziest movement of all was Dada, started by Tristan TZARA (1886–1963), Hugo BALL (1886–1927), and others, at the Cabaret Voltaire, Zurich, 1914. Not exactly a "theater" movement, it nevertheless used performance as a weapon. And what a weapon it turned out to be!*

Jarry's grotesque, self-important Père Ubu is captured in his friend Joan Miró's Surrealist painting. Ubu symbolized the greed of bourgeois society.

A hero of Tzara's was *Alfred* JARRY (1873–1907), the creator of one of the most important and devastatingly prophetic portrayals of despotism, Père Ubu, in his Shakespearean parody, *Ubu Roi* (1896). *Ubu* played only twice (riots closed the theater) but has remained an icon of anarchist theater.

Bourgeois audiences were invited to soirées only to have abuse, irony, satire, bombastic "art" declarations, and sometimes furniture hurled at them! The Dadaists even did it in the streets and frightened the horses. Initially a reaction to World War I, Dada preshadows the Existentialists, the 1960s "happenings," and the punk aesthetic as a signifier of the trademark sense of chaos, cynicism, and brutality of the 20th century. A more formally political version of Dada appeared in Berlin in 1916.

### War Protests

The Berlin Dada activities were aimed specifically at German involvement in the war. At the first "exhibition" of performance, sculpture, and painting, the cartoonist George Grosz dressed some pig carcasses in the uniform of the kaiser's troops and hung them from the ceiling. He was in prison before he could say "That's Dada, Volks!"

**1912** On its maiden voyage from Southampton to New York, the S.S. *Titanic* strikes an iceberg and sinks.

**1917** French composer Erik Satie's ballet *Parade* is performed with décor by Pablo Picasso and libretto by Jean Cocteau.

**1926** German filmmaker Fritz Lang and his scriptwriter wife Thea von Harbou make *Metropolis*, a movie about a futuristic city state.

Several "modernist" writers, although seemingly more mainstream, were influenced by Dadaist thinking. *Federico* GARCÍA LORCA (1898–1936) and *Luigi* PIRANDELLO (1867–1936) experimented with many styles, including Surrealism, fantasy, and farce. García Lorca is mostly remembered for his passionate peasant trilogy *Blood Wedding* (1933), *Yerma* (1934), and *The House of Bernarda Alba* (1936). But he also wrote *The Prodigious Shoemaker's Wife* (1926), a puppet-like farce, and *As Five Years Pass By* (1929), a Surrealist play within the mind of a man about to die. García Lorca was murdered by Spanish Falangists at the age of 38.

**PROMPT BOX**

Jarry was 15 when he wrote *Ubu Roi*. He intended it for puppets, and even when it reached the stage he wanted actors to be "puppetlike." Later he wrote three other "Ubu" plays before virtually becoming Ubu, riding around Paris on a bicycle with pistols strapped to his belt. He drank himself to death at 34. I blame the parents (and the bartenders).

**Learn Your Lines**

Jarry's views on audiences: "There are . . . at least two: that of the intelligent, small in number, and that of large number . . . ."

And on theater: Two things are ". . . notoriously horrid . . . and . . . encumber the stage uselessly: . . . the scenery and the actors."

He wanted mere placards to state location, and actors wearing masks and using monotone voices. Had they ever met, he and Craig would have gotten along well.

Pirandello was a skeptical pessimist (his wife was barking mad) and obsessed with the relationship between (fixed) art and (fluid) life. His best known work, *Six Characters in Search of an Author* (1921), initially caused uproar. But we now see it as a seminal modernist attack on traditional theater and bourgeois European values. You know the sort of thing.

*Oskar* SCHLEMMER (1888–1943), a German sculptor and director of the Bauhaus Theater, attempted to design theater from an abstract point of view, using costumes in geometric shapes to create "moving architecture." His ideas were realized in the Triadic Ballet, 1912–22, where dancers were attired in geometrically shaped costumes—and looked interesting, if a little silly.

Schlemmer's Triadic Ballet characters were defined according to his theories of shapes and colors.

**1917** Lenin hates smoking and bans all cigarettes from the train that takes him to St. Petersburg to initiate the Bolshevik Revolution.

**1921** France makes abortion illegal to compensate for all the population lost during the Great War.

**1931** Alfred M. Butts invents "Criss-Cross," a game played with wooden tiles on a board. James Brunot will take it over, name it Scrabble—and win.

1917~1939

# Experiments Between Lenin and Hitler

## Meyerhold, Piscator, Brecht

*In the early twentieth century, Europe overflowed with new forms and approaches to that old business of mincing around in funny clothes. No, I'm not talking about the armed forces or the Church (or their off-duty attire), but theater, dahlings, theater!*

**Behind the Scenes**
Technical innovations should never be an end in themselves, said Piscator. Stage design should "elevate the events on the stage onto a historical plane," and not just enlarge the technical range of machinery. "This elevation ... [is] ... inextricably bound up with the use of Marxist dialectics," and "my ... devices ... [are]... developed to cover up the deficiencies of the dramatists' products ..." (ouch!).

In Russia the genius *Vsevolod MEYERHOLD* (1874–1940) explored several styles of theater, all with extraordinary effect. At the Moscow Art Theater in 1905, Stanislavsky put him in charge of his new Studio and invited him to experiment with nonnaturalistic forms. Influenced by Oriental theater, Meyerhold, like Craig, believed that the essence of theater lay in movement and its difference from reality, not an imitation of it. Stan didn't like this at all, so Meyerhold went elsewhere and, under the pseudonym "Dr. Dapertutto," explored commedia dell'arte, circus, pantomime, and puppets. After Lenin, he moved on to revolutionary theater and Constructivism, trained his actors in the science of biomechanics, and finally explored socialist realism. But, from being one of the most revered artists in Russia, he fell foul of Stalinist thinking and was murdered in 1940 (his wife was butchered, too). Joe was never too much of an art lover.

Meyerhold's set for *Tarelkin's Death*, 1922: a "machine for acting."

One of the most significant creative forces in Germany was *Erwin* PISCATOR (1893–1966). He developed a kind of political agitprop style that incorporated film, photography, recorded voice, and live action into a montage theater. His revealing of the means of production (all the backstage stuff normally concealed by the proscenium arch) denied illusion. Overall, his trail-blazing in what came to be called epic theater (see box below) influenced Brecht, with whom he collaborated to produce *Rasputin* in 1927.

*Caucasian Chalk Circle* performed at London's National Theater in 1997.

*Bertolt* BRECHT (1898–1956) became the most influential writer/director in the West since World War II. His theories, as much as his plays, have created a template for non-illusionist political theater, especially "alienation," that much-abused term (see box). His many texts, including the Expressionist *Baal* (1919), *The Threepenny Opera* (1928), *The Life of Galileo* (1938), *Mother Courage* (1939), and, perhaps his best, *The Caucasian Chalk Circle* (1948), are revived endlessly. To escape the Nazis he fled to the U.S., but left in 1948 to escape McCarthyism and established the Berliner Ensemble theater with his wife, the actress Hélène Weigel.

**Alienation**

The "alienation effect" or, to use the German, *Verfremdungseffekt*, was Brecht's way of stopping actors from identifying with their roles, and demonstrating them instead. He used devices to distance the audience, such as having the actors whisper asides or wear strange masks. The technique, known as "epic theater," thus relied on audiences' reflective skills to interpret the action. Brechtophile directors, eager to copy the master, made this device something of a thespian buzzword. It wouldn't have gone over at all well with Method actors.

**1926** Recuperating from an addiction to opium, French dramatist, film director, artist, and poet Jean Cocteau writes his tragedy *Orphée*.

**1935** The employer of Carson McCullers, disturbed to find her reading Proust during office hours, dismisses her summarily.

**1940** Imprisoned for entering Britain without a visa, Arthur Koestler "would mark Pentonville with three stars. It is the most decent jail I have been in."

1925~1970

# Happiness Is ... a Good Thrashing

## The Ecstasy and Cruelty of Artaud and Grotowsky

*Whatever else they may be, visionaries tend not to be very practical. In* The Jet of Blood *by the Frenchman Antonin ARTAUD (1896–1948), one stage direction calls for the genuine hand of God to appear! I bet that pleased the stage manager. And one wonders how the acting of God affected insurance policies.*

Antonin Artaud in *The Passion of Saint Joan*, 1928. The eyes say it all.

An uncompromising man, Artaud founded the Théâtre Alfred Jarry (see page 106) in 1927, having been thrown out of the Surrealist movement for being too extreme (get the picture?). His notion of theater as an act of cruelty (which became infamous in London during the 1960s via Charles Marowitz's "Theater of Cruelty" season) was a huge influence on European and American avant-garde theater. He didn't mean physical cruelty to the actors (unfortunately) but a spectacle of violence and sexuality to offend the audience out of their complacency. In 1938 he codified these thoughts in a seminal work, *The Theater and Its Double*, where the "double" of theater was real life. To him, what was needed to combat the word-dominated rhetorical theater was a "poetry of space" filled with music, dance, painting, chanting,

### How Not to Act

Jerzy Grotowsky said acting was "... a process of self-revelation, going back as far as the subconscious," and the construction of a score "whose notes are ... what we call 'give and take.' We ... do not teach him [sic] how to create [for example, how to play Hamlet] ... for it is ... in this 'how' that the seeds of banality and ... clichés that defy creation are planted." Food for thought, don't you think?

### Behind the Scenes

From Artaud's *Theater of Cruelty Manifesto* (1932): "We intend to do away with the stage and auditorium, replacing them with a ... single, undivided locale without any partitions of any kind ... Direct contact will be established between ... actors and audience." Theater architecture should be a "barn or hangar" like "some churches, holy places, or certain Tibetan temples."

**1951** The American government carries out above-ground nuclear tests in the Nevada desert; hundreds of square miles are contaminated.

**1958** In Ethiopia, locusts consume a million pounds' worth of grain.

**1970** American rock-blues singer Janis Joplin dies of a heroin overdose at the age of 27; she is one of the first white singers to achieve success with the blues.

## *Supporting Roles*

*Artaud founded the Théâtre Alfred Jarry with* **Roger Vitrac** *(1899–1952), a Dadaist who wrote at least one excellent Surrealist play,* Victor *or* Power to the Children *(1928). This was a satire with a grotesque nine-year-old protagonist (he was six feet tall, for a start!) who was able to see straight through the pretensions and hypocrisy of bourgeois values and patriotism. Vitrac's subsequent plays were flops and he gave up theater. Oh, the fickleness of the paying, theatergoing public!*

and gesture. He envisaged a model for theater based on "a police raid on brothels"; "theater was to be like the plague from which people would emerge either dead or purged." Predictably, most of his later years were spent in an asylum.

In Poland, at his Theater of 13 Rows (in Opole) and later in his Teatr Laboritorium, *Jerzy* GROTOWSKY (1933–1999) trained his actors to enter a trance state wherein it is rumored some could slow their own heartbeat and produce welts on the skin during mimed flagellation scenes. Influenced by Artaud, he also wanted a radical theater of poetry that would transform the actor-audience relationship. His was a "poor" theater without makeup, costume, décor, stage, lights, or sound effects: the only necessary elements were "an actor and a spectator." (However, every single production he did, including Goethe's *Faust*, Mickiewicz's *Forefather's Eve*, and Wyspiansky's *Acropolis*, carried production credits for direction, costume, properties, and design. Hmm!)

Grotowsky outside his Teatr Laboritorium in 1966.

Grotowsky's major work, *Toward a Poor Theater*, was as thorough a guide to acting as were the writings of Stanislavsky—it just didn't catch on quite as well. Perhaps he overlooked the fact that people generally go to the theater to enjoy themselves.

Peter Brook's *Marat/Sade*, 1964: his turn to do some Theater of Cruelty.

**1944** Anne Frank's family is betrayed to the Gestapo after more than two years in hiding.

**1947** Buckminster Fuller develops the geodesic dome. He will develop geodesics, the mathematical study of economical space-spanning structures.

**1950** The body of a man ritually murdered in about 240 B.C. is discovered in a peat bog in Denmark; Professor P. V. Glob's *The Bog People* investigates this and other similar grisly finds.

1944~1961

# Meanwhile, in Life's Waiting Room

## Existentialism

*Existentialism, or "heroic pessimism," is a philosophy that developed in France after World War II as a response to a meaningless world in which freedom of choice is denied. Since each person is thus a "free agent" trying to control his or her life, personal experience and responsibility are all-important.*

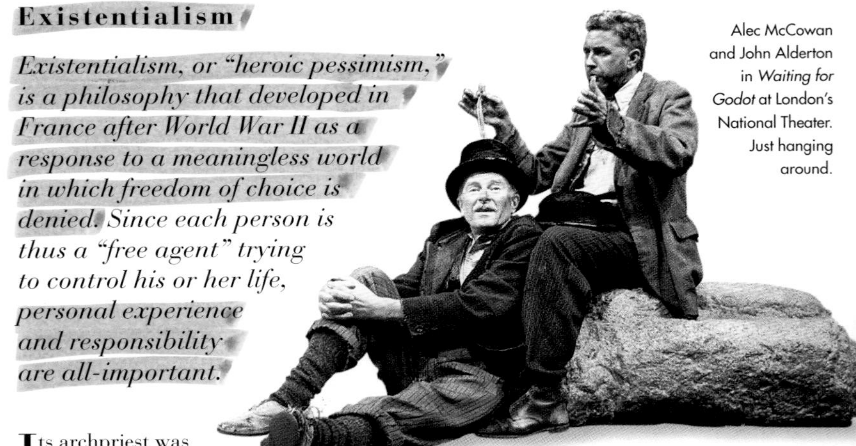

Alec McCowan and John Alderton in *Waiting for Godot* at London's National Theater. Just hanging around.

Its archpriest was *Jean-Paul SARTRE* (1905–80), who, in plays like *The Flies* (1943) and *No Exit* (1944), attempted to invent a "theater of situations" where actions define characters rather than any psychological state. *Albert CAMUS* (1913–60), another Existentialist, wrote *Caligula* (1945) and *The Just* (1949). Frankly, both wrote better novels and

archpriest was *Jean-Paul SARTRE* (1905–80), who, in plays like *The Flies* (1943) and *No Exit* (1944), attempted to invent a "theater of situations" where actions define characters rather than any psychological state. *Albert CAMUS* (1913–60), another Existentialist, wrote *Caligula* (1945) and *The Just* (1949). Frankly, both wrote better novels
and essays. Their plays were mostly long-winded public debates.

Possibly the greatest writer and thinker to emerge this century was the Irishman *Samuel BECKETT* (1906–89). What Sartre and Camus couldn't resolve theatrically, Beckett did with consummate brilliance.

Beckett's principal works, from *Waiting*

**PROMPT BOX**

Beckett's love of music hall is evident in his characters and their situations. The comedian's sense of desperation to keep going to the bitter end, no matter what the audience response, is echoed by Beckett's characters as they wait, struggle to remember, or try to find purpose in their existence. It's as if he sees the clown's act as a metaphor for all our lives.

**1949** French philosopher, essayist, novelist, and partner of Jean-Paul Sartre, Simone de Beauvoir publishes her feminist essay *Le Deuxième sexe (The Second Sex)*.

**1955** The millionth Volkswagen "beetle" rolls off the production line.

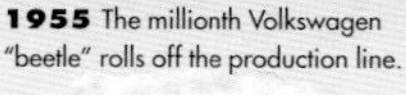

**1961** Soviet cosmonaut Yuri Gagarin is the first human in space; in a flight lasting only two hours, his tiny space capsule circles the earth at a maximum altitude of 187 miles.

(some are silent), deed (sometimes characters literally do nothing), and setting (they are located "nowhere," with a minimalist set). They are, somehow, magically, also superb theater.

Camus once described human existence as "absurd," which helped the critic Martin Esslin title his book *The Theater of the Absurd* (1961). One of its inclusions was the half-French, half-Romanian *Eugène* IONESCO (b. 1912), whose first play, *The Bald Soprano* (1950), was inspired by reading English phrase books. With story and characterization replaced by surreal and hallucinatory events, it perfectly mirrors the crazy world we live in. Subsequent one-act plays, *The Lesson* (1951), *The Chairs* (1952), and *Rhinoceros* (1960), placed him as one of France's top theater-writing talents. They are successful, possibly because they don't forget to be funny.

**Behind the Scenes**
During World War II many European theaters were destroyed. Germany began to rebuild and produce immediately (they also improvised with some of the huge stages of the old opera buildings). In Britain, old theaters fell into decline, but the rise of the Arts Council funded a growing repertory movement. In the U.S., the new university provided regional centers for theater.

### *Supporting Roles*

**Jean Genet** *(1910–86), poet, novelist, and playwright, made his name writing homoerotic novels while in prison. He revolutionized theater with five plays including* The Maids *(1947)*, The Balcony *(1956), and* The Blacks *(1959). Highly theatrical, his plays reveal the abuses of power, and suggest that all social roles exist partly to deceive.*

William Sabatier, Jean-Louis Barrault, and Simone Velere in *Rhinoceros*, 1960.

**1954** Ray Kroc visits Mac and Dick MacDonald's hamburger stand in San Bernardino California; his chain of fast-food restaurants based on their model will earn him $600,000,000.

**1955** American drama critic Walter Kerr publishes *How Not to Write a Play*; "the fun-loving American finds the theater infinitely resistible—and at any price."

**1959** Glen Raven Mills of Altamahaw, N.C., introduces pantyhose—waist-high nylons requiring no additional support.

1947~1990s

# The American Method

## (Or How I Stopped Acting and Learned to Mumble)

Life membership in the American club.

*In 1947, Elia Kazan and others from the Group Theater (see below) founded a workshop called the Actors' Studio. It charged no fees, was not a school, and anyone who got past the tough audition was a member for life. Since then, everyone who is anyone in American theater and film has been a member, from Marlon Brando to Ellen Burstyn and Dustin Hoffman. In 1963 the Studio opened its own theater on Broadway, although this closed shortly after.*

When Group member *Lee Strasberg* (1901–82) took over artistic direction in 1951, the Studio became home to a "shrug and mumble" school of acting known as the Method. Founded on the least interesting part of Stanislavsky's work (the bit that goes on about psychology and the actor's "emotional memory"—see page 88), the Method unforgivably persuaded actors that what they feel is basically all that matters. (And they don't need much encouragement to think that!) In so doing, it elevated the actor to undeserved heights of neurotic self-importance while lowering acting to equally undeserved depths of self-indulgent mannerism.

Lee Strasberg offering tips on Method acting.

### Supporting Roles

**Cheryl Crawford** *(1902–86) cofounded the Group Theater, and later the Actors' Studio. Always seen as the steadying influence within the Group, she kept the peace between Clurman and Strasberg (whom she referred to as "Old Testament prophets"). After she left the Group she independently produced musicals, such as* Brigadoon *(1947) and* Paint Your Wagon *(1950), as well as plays.*

**1961** About 1,500 Cuban exiles, backed by the CIA, fail in their attempt to overthrow the Cuban president, Fidel Castro; the Bay of Pigs fiasco further sours Cuba's relationship with the U.S.

**1995** 32-year-old American film director Quentin Tarantino's *Pulp Fiction* is a heady blend of violence, comedy, and gloss.

**1997** Boxing star Mike Tyson, convicted of rape in 1992, bites off a chunk of opponent Evander Holyfield's ear; Tyson is disqualified and Holyfield's ear repaired by surgery.

Brando oozing the hormone testosterone and mastication in *Streetcar*.

Note the "realistically grubby, " though painted, setting.

In 1934, when the brilliant actor, teacher, and Group member Stella Adler returned from working with Stanislavsky in Paris to pass on his reaffirmation of "character" as essential to dramatic action (and thus acting as essentially a pretense), Strasberg metaphorically put his fingers in his ears and sang loudly. Nevertheless, the Method went on to become the quintessential style in 20th-century American theater and (especially) in Realist film.

The director *Elia Kazan* (b. 1909) produced new American Realist plays and films of, for example, *A Streetcar Named Desire* (1947), *Death of a Salesman* (1949), and *Cat on a Hot Tin Roof* (1955) in a highly naturalistic "Method" style, full of intense feelings, emotions, and brooding sexuality (most of which were put there by the playwrights).

Liz Taylor plots how to seduce her husband in *Cat on a Hot Tin Roof*.

**PROMPT BOX**

Of the actors associated with the Method, Marlon Brando (b. 1924) is the most famous. His first notable appearance was in Elia Kazan's stage production of *Streetcar*. Dustin Hoffman (b. 1937) carried on the tradition in *Death of a Salesman*, as did Ellen Burstyn in *Same Time, Next Year* (1975). The rest, as they say, is history.

**1925** Irish playwright George Bernard Shaw is awarded the Nobel Prize for Literature but refuses to accept it, for political reasons.

**1932** Typographic consultant Stanley Morison's new typeface "Times New Roman" gives Britain's longest-running newspaper, *The Times*, a more contemporary look.

**1937** Shirley Temple and her American studio receive damages of $9,800 after British novelist Graham Greene suggests in an article that her older male fans find the little star's appearance titillating.

1925~1956

# Stiff Upper Lip, Crease in Your Flannels
## (Or a Creased Upper Lip and a Stiff in Your Flannels?)

*The period between the wars and up to the "watershed" year of 1956 (when* Look Back in Anger *was performed; see page 120) was a kind of theatrical playtime in England. Having had little contact with Expressionism, Dada, Futurism, etc. (but aware of them), and in contrast to any politically motivated revolutionary or post-revolutionary European theater, English drama focused on social comedies, farces, or mildly controversial "Realist" plays about social ills or World War II. Naturalism and traditional 19th-century staging dominated, and Shaw was still king, of course.*

Coward's plays could hardly be called innovative.

Noel trips the light fantastic with Gertrude Lawrence in *Private Lives*.

*Noel COWARD* (1899–1973) was known as "The Master" in theatrical circles (but Master of what?). His plays, from *Fallen Angels* (1925) through *Hay Fever* (1925) and *Private Lives* (1930) to *This Happy Breed* (1942), and the even worse *Peace in Our Time* (1947), were at best slight, brittle comedies of bourgeois manners and at worst rather nauseating patriotism. His was a reactionary, flag-waving world where the rich were jolly fine people and the poor had the decency to know their place. The 1920s weren't called frivolous for nothing! Coward also wrote some ditties and tunes and was awarded a knighthood in 1970.

*Terence RATTIGAN* (1911–77) was another writer of weightless comedies, such as *French Without Tears* (1936). He got a bit serious with *Flare Path* (1942), about his wartime experiences, and dipped a toe

**1939** King George VI and Queen Elizabeth, on a visit to Canada and the United States, eat hot dogs with President and Mrs. Franklin Roosevelt.

**1954–55** English philologist and specialist in Old Norse language and literature J. R. R. Tolkien publishes his fantasy trilogy, *The Lord of the Rings*, which will achieve cult status.

**1956** British antinuclear protesters march from the Aldermaston research station to London.

## Supporting Roles

*There were some exceptions to the theater of "toffs" and "gels."* **Joan Littlewood** *(b. 1914) and* **Ewan MacColl** *(1915–89) founded the experimental, left-wing Theater Union in 1935, which paved the way for the agit-prop theaters of the 1960s. Influenced by German political theater, Littlewood directed many controversial plays and pioneered the medium of documentary drama. Her most famous production was* Oh, What a Lovely War! *(1963).*

into social realism with *The Winslow Boy* (1946), about a miscarriage of justice. His most well known play is *Separate Tables* (1954), a study of the psychological impact of cravat and flannels on a tweed two-piece suit. He was knighted in 1971.

*Separate Tables:* a tale of emotional inadequacy in a seaside hotel.

*R[obert]. C[edric]. SHERRIFF* (1896–1975) wrote several plays but only *Journey's End* (1928), an angry and realistic portrayal of soldiers at the front line, was any good. Shaw called it "a useful corrective to the romantic conception of war." The farceur *Ben TRAVERS* (1886–1980) had ten of his comedies put on at the Aldwych Theater from 1925 to 1933. These became known as the "Aldwych farces," and included *A Cuckoo in the Nest* (1925), *Rookery Nook* (1926), and *Dirty Work* (1932). His last farce, *The Bed Before Yesterday*, was written and staged when he was 89 years old.

**Behind the Scenes**

Of course, the biggest crowd-puller of the time were the "talking-pictures," and the wireless was very popular too. Music hall still had some life in it via Max Miller, George Robey, and Gracie Fields, but television finally nailed it firmly into its coffin. Live entertainment now lives on in comedy and variety shows, and in rock concerts.

**1937** American pioneering aviator Amelia Earhart and her plane, the *Flying Laboratory*, set off to fly around the world; they disappear over the Pacific Ocean.

**1938** Austrian psychoanalyst Sigmund Freud, 82, takes refuge from Nazi Austria and moves to London.

**1945** Dissatisfaction with commercial theater leads Joan Littlewood and others to found the Theater Workshop; from 1953, the company will be based at the Theater Royal at Stratford in East London.

1930~1970

# Keep One's Vowels Regular!

## Gielgud, Richardson, Olivier

*Who needs Russian Constructivism, Italian Surrealism, German Expressionism, Piscator, Brecht, or even the American "Method" when it's perfectly obvious that real theater needs only a bit of aristocratic elegance and perfect diction? If American acting was "shrug and mumble," in England it became all "head and voice," where nothing moved from the neck down.*

**PROMPT BOX**

Donald Wolfit (1902–68), the last actor-manager, loved to give really good value for money. He spent many years touring "classical" roles, and one of his best was as Oedipus in *Oedipus Rex*. Ever the showman, he would shock and delight audiences when Oedipus "put out his eyes" by staggering from the wings with two peeled red grapes sliding down his face.

And to those philistines who complain that such acting is antitheatrical, stultifyingly dull, and has the physically expressive range of a wooden plank, or that a pretentiously aristocratic English accent that ignores the richness of the regions, not to mention Scotland, Ireland, or Wales, reduces theater to a snobbish, elitist pastime, the only response is a contemptuous gaze, flared nostrils, and a single arched eyebrow. How dare they! For what can be more spiritually uplifting or theatrically exciting than a fencepost spellbinding us with mellifluous, rounded tones? (What? I say, steady on, old man!)

*Sir John* GIELGUD (b. 1904) began knocking audiences off their plush seats in 1924 as Trofimov in *The Cherry Orchard*. He has gone on to ever-greater things at the Old Vic and just about every major theater since. His most famous role is that of Hamlet, which he produced himself in 1933, and, apart from championing Shakespeare, he has helped make Chekhov agreeable to the English by producing adaptations of his plays.

*Ralph* RICHARDSON (1902–83) was better made for contemporary

Sir John Gielgud's Hamlet (1934), looking more fed up than royally troubled.

**1949** English journalist, essayist, and novelist George Orwell publishes *Nineteen Eighty-Four*, a chilling futuristic fable of totalitarianism.

**1963** John Gielgud: "Good verse-speaking is rather like swimming. If you surrender to the water it keeps you up, but if you fight you drown."

**1968** Billie Jean King is the first American woman in 28 years to win all major tennis competitions in Britain and the United States.

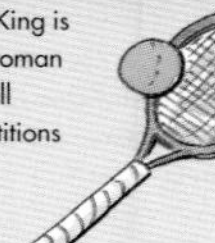

Olivier as Archie Rice (1957) captures in his rictus the desperation of fading music hall.

## Supporting Roles

*Actors* **Paul Scofield** *(b. 1922)*, **Emlyn Williams** *(1905–87)*, **Charles Laughton** *(1899–1962), and* **Michael Redgrave** *(1908–85) all developed their talents in either the Old Vic or Stratford-Upon-Avon. Directors, too, like* **Tyrone Guthrie** *(1900–71), and foreign imports* **Michel Saint-Denis** *(1897–1971) and* **Fyodor Komissarzhevsky** *(1882–1954) helped the Vic become one of the most important theaters in England.*

plays than Shakespeare. He excelled in "ordinary" parts where he could display his natural sense of gentle innocence and fair play. Plays by Somerset Maugham and J. B. Priestley, especially the latter's *Johnson over Jordan* (1939), were perfect. Later in his illustrious career he specialized in playing a selection of quaintly eccentric bumblers in theater and film.

In 1970, *Laurence OLIVIER* (1907–89) was the first actor ever to be made a Lord (what next? president? ... oh yes, I forgot). A Shakespearean actor, he also played contemporary parts, such as Archie Rice in John Osborne's *The Entertainer* (1957). He was a movie actor and the first director of the English National Theater in 1963. His physical agility, a "just get on with it" approach to acting, and somewhat eccentric diction separated him from his peers. His response to Dustin Hoffman's aggressive Method preparation for his role in *Marathon Man* is classic: "But dear boy, why don't you just *act* it?"

**Dame It!**

Edith Evans (1888–1976), Peggy Ashcroft (1907–91), Flora Robson (1902–84), and Joan Plowright (b. 1929) were fellow performers of the boys mentioned above. Joan Plowright married Olivier in 1961. The other three became Dames, and Peggy had a theater in the suburb of Croydon, south of London, named after her (a somewhat backhanded compliment).

Dame Flora Robson (in 1935), mistress of the level stare that was not to be tangled with.

**1956** Despite having had no formal coach, and training for only one hour a day, 25-year-old medical student from Oxford University Roger Bannister breaks the running record of four minutes to the mile.

**1959** *One Way Pendulum* by English playwright N. F. Simpson is a rare example in Britain of the Theater of the Absurd.

**1962** Decca Records turns down the opportunity to sign up the Beatles in favor of a recording deal with Brian Poole and the Tremolos.

1956~1970

# Reviving the Corpse

## Osborne, Devine, Wesker, Ayckbourn

On a soap box.

*The year 1956 has been called a watershed for British theater, mainly because the play* Look Back in Anger, *by John* OSBORNE *(1929–94), seemed to signal a revival in English drama (which was almost flatlining!). While this is true, it certainly overrates Osborne's play, which centers on Jimmy Porter, a working-class, university-educated boy whose rants against middle-class society led to the phrase "angry young man" (subsequently applied to any artist critical of society). But Porter's anger is more of a whine, and he is as reactionary as those he attacks, guilty of material jealousy, and weak misogyny.*

**PROMPT BOX**

Brecht's influence got through to Britain by the 1960s. Joan Littlewood had, of course, noticed it long before, but she was very special. In 1960, the writer Robert Bolt (b. 1924) created *A Man for All Seasons*, starring Paul Scofield. In this he used the "Brechtian" devices of a narrator and an episodic structure.

Two angry young men: John Osborne (right) with Ken Hough, who played the original Jimmy Porter in *Look Back in Anger*, at the Royal Court, 1956.

More important was the vision of *George* DEVINE (1910–65), whose English Stage Company (formed 1954) produced Osborne's plays at the Royal Court Theater, and was committed to changing the conditions of theater in England by new work. Devine helped many new writers and actors find their feet (it's an old theatrical problem—not knowing where your feet are).

One of those writers was *Arnold* WESKER (b. 1932), who, although critically attacked, has often shown more bravery and adventure in his writing than many others and, unlike Osborne, was one of the

**1963** The jawbone of *Zinjanthropus*, a manlike creature who lived two million years ago, is found at Lake Natron in Tanzania.

**1969** British troops are sent into Northern Ireland after Protestant-Catholic riots; only in 1998 does the political situation allow the possibility of their permanent withdrawal.

**1970** British poet Ted Hughes publishes *Crow*, a sequence of poems with illustrations by Leonard Baskin; its darkness and bleakness will influence subsequent British poetry.

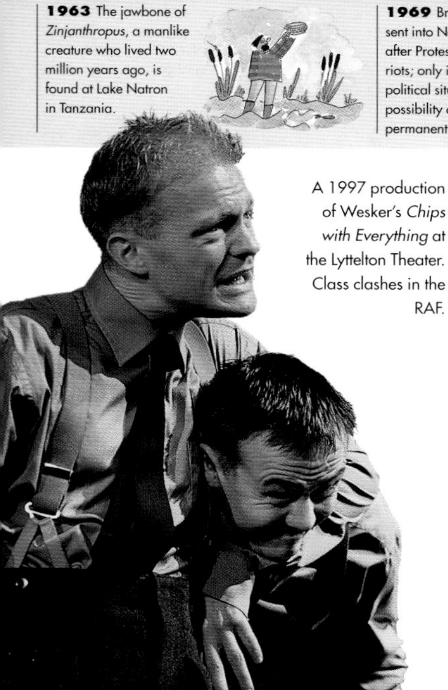

A 1997 production of Wesker's *Chips with Everything* at the Lyttelton Theater. Class clashes in the RAF.

few genuine working-class writers. Wesker's early works, such as *Roots* (1959) and *Chips with Everything* (1962), helped articulate the working-class socialist hopes that followed the war.

The incredible popularity of *Alan Ayckbourn* (b. 1939) guaranteed academic and critical indifference for years, for it is a very English (if tiresome and stupid) intellectual snobbery to equate success with poor quality. And successful he is, outstripped in terms of international translations and popularity only by Shakespeare. His plays premiered at Scarborough because, as he sensibly says, theater is "like bingo, just somewhere to go when it's raining" (if a little more expensive than bingo). From *Relatively Speaking* (1967) onward, his plays demonstrate technical acrobatics with incredibly sharp observations of the middle class, using comedy to illuminate the small, if frighteningly claustrophobic, tragedies of life. The *Norman Conquests* trilogy (1974) shows simultaneous events in the dining room, living room, and backyard of a house one weekend. Theatrically he taps into that modern sense of futile absurdity first articulated by Sartre and Camus—only with jokes.

**Behind the Scenes**

Ayckbourn's method for writing plays is a lesson in how to get on with it! To avoid facing the "tyranny of the blank page" for too long, he creates an annual program for his Steven Joseph Theater in Scarborough to include a new Ayckbourn play, titled, but not yet written! He then has to write it before the season starts! But one still wonders if he procrastinates to the very last minute . . .

Looking for the muse.

## Supporting Roles

**John Arden** *(b. 1930), famous for* Sergeant Musgrave's Dance *(1959) and* Live Like Pigs *(1957), now lives in Ireland and prefers to write for non-professional theaters.* **Ann Jellicoe** *(b. 1927), whose* The Sport of My Mad Mother *(1956) explored nonliterary speech rhythms, went on to write* The Knack *(1961). She has long been a supporter of community drama.*

**1954** Food rationing ends in Britain and ration books are burned at Conservative Associations all across the country.

**1960** A small family-run shoe manufacturer in rural England introduces a chunky, eyelet-laced utility boot with a cushioned sole called "Dr. Martens" after their German inventor, Dr. Klaus Maertens.

**1963** In Britain, an armed gang hijacks a train (which is carrying bank notes for incineration) and escapes with more than £2.5 million.

1954~1973

# Angry Young Persons

## The Revolutionaries

*While Jimmy Porter ranted, other writers in Europe and the U.S. were demonstrating a more focused and real anger, though not always politically motivated, and preparing the ground for the 1960s' arts "revolutions."*

### Supporting Roles

**Shelagh Delaney** *(b. 1939) wrote the great* A Taste of Honey *(1958) when she was 17.* Saved *(1965), by* **Edward Bond** *(b. 1934), brought British stage censorship crashing down. The controversial scene of a baby being stoned in a pram was his angry attempt to reflect the moral mayhem of contemporary life. Bond claimed: "I write about violence as Jane Austen wrote about manners. Violence shapes and obsesses our society..."*

Harold PINTER (b. 1930) was influenced by Beckett. His early work, like *The Birthday Party* (1958), revealed a similar interest in the terror of torment without reason, and *The Caretaker* (1960) has much in common with Beckett's *Waiting for Godot* in its use of a tramp to signify pointless existence (or to signify that life was all about the struggle to get to Sidcup). For years he put "silence" and "noncommunication" on stage in a big way, but after *Betrayal* (1978), he seems to have changed his style to a more straightforward storytelling.

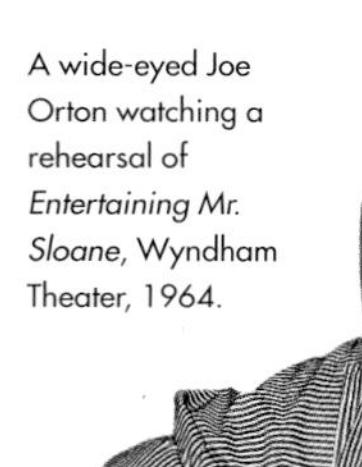

A wide-eyed Joe Orton watching a rehearsal of *Entertaining Mr. Sloane*, Wyndham Theater, 1964.

*Joe ORTON* (1933–67) rejoiced in defacing library books, promiscuity, and brilliant, bizarre, and very funny plays with arch dialogue. From *Entertaining Mr. Sloane* (1964), he theatrically said the unsayable. His funniest play, *What the Butler Saw* (1969), works as a farce, a Wildean comedy, and a satire of psychiatry. Sadly, he was murdered by his talentless and jealous lover, Kenneth Halliwell, who then committed suicide.

**1964** When Joe Orton's *Entertaining Mr. Sloane* transfers to a theater in London's West End, it is attacked both for being highbrow and a commercial success.

**1968** Soviet tanks roll into the Czech capital, putting an end to the economic and political reforms introduced by Alexander Dubcek; the "Prague Spring" is over.

**1973** German-born British economist E. F. Schumacher's *Small is beautiful*: "Man is small, and, therefore, small is beautiful. To go for giantism is to go for self-destruction."

The brilliant Leonard Rossiter in Orton's *Loot* (1965), which premiered in Brighton.

*Dario Fo* (b. 1926), once an established writer/comedian in cabaret, television, and mildly satiric plays, realized with horror during the 1960s that his plays were enjoyed by those he sought to pillory. So with his wife, Franca Rame, he formed his own company, Nuova Scena, and later, La Commune, to revive genuine working-class theater exposing corruption and oppression. Since going for the jugular he has become famous internationally as a comic mime and writer with plays like *Accidental Death of an Anarchist* (1970) and *Mistero Buffo* (1967), explorations of corrupt ideology and human weakness.

**Borstal Boy**
Brendan Behan (1923–64), an IRA member who had served time in prison, was made famous by Joan Littlewood when she produced his comic account of a prisoner waiting to hang in *The Quare Fellow* (1956). *Borstal Boy* (1958) documented his own time behind bars. He belonged to the same tradition as Sean O'Casey, but unfortunately drank himself to death at the age of 41.

The Afro-American *Amiri Baraka* (born Leroi Jones, 1934) became a leader of the 1960s black arts political movement. His plays, for example, *Dutchman* (1964), *The Slave* (1964), and *Slave Ship* (1967), display his "fierce and blazing talent" and strong antiwhite feeling. He has had a great influence on black American theater.

Out of the postwar Women's Liberation Movement came a "Feminist theater" fighting sexism in society. Always radical, in most cases feminist art was suffocated by self-righteous politics, but some groups channeled agitprop anger beyond hectoring into sophisticated theater. An injection of humor is usually all it takes.

Angry black theater generation meets angry black movie generation: Amiri Baraka (center) and Spike Lee, director of the movie *Malcolm X* (right).

**1947** The radio quiz show *You Bet Your Life* has Groucho Marx ad-libbing interviews with guests; translated to the small screen in 1951, it wins an Emmy Award as the funniest show on TV.

**1955** Disneyland, the amusement park that is also a vacation destination, opens its doors and proves to be Walt Disney's greatest success.

**1956** Arthur Miller is subpoenaed to appear before the House Committee on Un-American Activities; he refuses to implicate other Communist writers and is fined for contempt.

1935~1985

# Tellin' It like It Is

## The American Realists

*One by one the Big Boys emerged with a new style of theater that wasn't afraid to get its hands dirty. In the politically turbulent American 1930s, Langston HUGHES's* Mulatta *put black issues by black writers and actors firmly on the stage. Tennessee WILLIAMS's steamy* A Glass Menagerie *premiered in 1945, and Arthur MILLER's keynote* Death of a Salesman *in 1949.*

Purveyor of social protest in poetry: Langston Hughes in 1967, the year of his death.

*The Glass Menagerie* by *Tennessee WILLIAMS* (1911–83) brought the tensions, heat, and suffocation of those poor souls who need booze'n'sex to cope (most people I know, actually) to an astonished and homophobic postwar stage. Two years later his genius was confirmed by *A Streetcar Named Desire*, featuring a glowering, sweaty Marlon Brando as Stanley Kowalski. Williams went on to write some of the finest lyrical theater ever produced in the U.S. in plays like *Cat on a Hot Tin Roof* (1955) and *Suddenly Last Summer* (1958), before declining in power and control. He was, apparently, overfond of intravenous amphetamines and casual sex—two activities one might have thought to be mutually exclusive, but not, according to rumor, in his case.

How to make a torn undershirt sexy. Brando fueling his angst in *Streetcar*.

**Behind the Scenes**

Movies were taking over in the U.S. in a big way. Talkies arrived in 1927, with the offensive *Jazz Singer*. Theaters declined by two-thirds in the 1920s as houses built screens, and Manhattan became the center for professional theater. Before the Depression, there were almost 300 shows on Broadway; ten years later there were only 80.

**1965** Government health warnings on cigarette packs are required by law in the United States.

**1973** Richard Nixon, in Disney World, denies involvement in the "Watergate Affair" and tells the American people that their president "is not a crook."

**1977** Elvis Presley, the king of rock 'n' roll, is found dead at his Memphis home; rumors of sightings of the King will abound for many years to come.

## Supporting Roles

***Neil Simon** (b. 1927) is probably the most successful playwright on Broadway. His output (almost a hit a year since 1961) and productions rival Ayckbourn in England. But critical acclaim doesn't come easy. He writes gags well and mild satires of middle-class mores, but his scalpel is not as sharp as Ayckbourn's, nor does it cut as deep. He remains, however, the master of the twinkle and the wry smile.*

*Arthur* MILLER (b. 1915) won the Pulitzer Prize with *Death of a Salesman*. Although basically a Realist play, it often shifted into Expressionist mode in telling the story of a failed commercial traveler. In 1953 he wrote *The Crucible*, ostensibly about the Salem witch trials, but actually responding to McCarthy's zealous "subversives" witch-hunt. Since the death of Williams, Miller has been called America's greatest living playwright.

Perhaps the most obscure American playwright is *Sam* SHEPARD (b. 1943). His output of over 40 plays reveals wide and diverse influences like rock and roll, drug culture, and dance, and he seems obsessed by myths of the West, the American Dream, and notions of "roots" (in other words, a typical American writer). From *The Rock Garden* (1964) to the brilliant *Fool for Love* (1979) and *True West* (1980), he has stretched the boundaries of the Realist form to accommodate cinematic and graphic art sensibilities.

Male bonding (with balls). Warren Mitchell (center) as Willy Loman in *Death of a Salesman*.

*David* MAMET (b. 1947) emerged in the 1970s with plays like *Sexual Perversity in Chicago* (a great name to get attention for your first play). In 1977, his *American Buffalo* proved him a writer of great characterization and naturalistic dialogue. *Glengarry Glen Ross* (1983) won the Pulitzer Prize for its tales of troubled Chicago realtors (and you must admit it takes real genius to make anyone care about realtors).

**1960** Joseph Beuys produces his sculpture *Bathtub*, the tub he used to bathe in as a child, covered in adhesive bandages and soaked in gauze.

**1966** The American TV network NBC premieres the science fiction series *Star Trek*, which will continue for 78 episodes and win cult status.

**1969** 400,000 young people attend a weekend pop festival near the artists' colony of Woodstock to hear 32 rock and folk groups.

1960~1975

# It's the Sixties! So Get Your Clothes Off!

## Hair and Happenings

Getting into *The Brig.*

*The 1960s were the time to "drop out" of a materialistic world, and change it for the better through drugs, sex, and good old rock'n'roll. Embarrassing though it may seem now, it was all taken very seriously then. And perhaps you may be forgiven for secretly thinking it was actually a good idea.*

In England, the same day as the Lord Chancellor's work ended as theater censor, the nude musical extravaganza *Hair* had its English premiere. Its impact was huge, but it was very much a product of its time. The script was terrible and, as Charles Marowitz commented, there was a certain "hippie mindlessness" beneath its surface. It was basically just an excuse for the actors to get naked in public.

*Hair* was a commercial version of another experiment: the Happening. The term was coined by the painter Allan Kaprow (sort of the originator), and is an event of calculated impermanence and spontaneity. A happening occurs once only and there is no beginning, middle, or end. In a happening there is no separation between actor and audience, no script, and much is left to chance (just like life, eh?).

*Hair* had been restaged from an original show by Tom O'Horgan from La Mama

**The Woosters**

A very influential theater was the Performance Group (now the Wooster Group) from New York. Under Richard Schechner, they produced *Dionysus in 69*, a total audience participation show (very 1960s) where everyone was asked to join in sexual activities with the cast and each other. Nice work if you can get it.

**1971** "Hot pants" become fashionable.

**1973** The longest solar eclipse in history is visible from the Southern Sahara desert.

**1974** A Swedish woman sues the Israeli psychic Uri Geller, known to TV audiences for his spoon-bending skills, for making her I.U.D. ineffective.

Experimental Theater Club (Café La Mama). Started by Ellen Stewart in 1962, La Mama became one of the most important American venues for new work, hosting Grotowsky, Peter Brook, Eugenio Barba, and others. La Mama was itself influenced by the eclectic activities of Julian Beck and Judith Malina and their Living Theater (which kicked off the Off-off Broadway theaters). Formed as a collective (which means no one does the dishes), theirs was a confrontational theater, often shouting in the faces of their audience about various social crimes (like, er . . . trying to leave the theater?). Influenced by Artaud, they saw themselves as "gurus" of a new American pacifist order. (But hey, Americans believe in the power of complaining!).

*Hair* also spawned imitators, including *Oh! Calcutta!* (1969), written by critic Kenneth Tynan (whose fame rested largely on being the very first person to say "fuck" on television. One wonders who will ever be the last?). He persuaded famous names (including John Lennon, Sam Shepard, Joe Orton, and even Sam Beckett) to write bits of pornography as part of the script while retaining their anonymity. But it was not a success critically, and at least one female critic complained that the male "members" in the cast remained disappointingly unaroused! Honestly, some people really insist on getting their money's worth at the theater.

## Supporting Roles

**Joseph Chaikin** *(b. 1935) worked with the Living Theater in the early 1960s and founded The Open Theater in 1964 as an experimental company. His approach was workshop-based, wherein actors continually tried new means of extending their art and improvising their dialogue and actions. He has directed many other theaters since, and his influence on modern American acting has been considerable.*

The 1967 production of *Hair* with cast looking like rejects from Village People auditions.

**PROMPT BOX**

The Living Theater ran into trouble for nonpayment of taxes to the IRS. The IRS closed their theater down in 1963 during a run of Kenneth Brown's *The Brig*. The last audiences had to climb in through the windows of the theater to see it (which no doubt guaranteed a good audience response: who would want to admit that such an effort had not been worthwhile?). After this the Living Theater exiled themselves in Europe before returning in 1968.

**1960** The world's first felt-tip pen is produced by a Japanese company.

**1963** President John F. Kennedy is assassinated in Dallas, Texas; Lee Harvey Oswald is subsequently arrested but is himself shot before being tried for the murder.

**1965** Unwilling to share power with Rhodesia's black citizens, Prime Minister Ian Smith signs the Unilateral Declaration of Independence from Great Britain.

1960~1979

# The Times, They Are A'Changin'

## Agitprop in the U.K.

*If aesthetic change was one side of the 1960s' "revolutionary coin," political change was the other. Agitprop (plays trying to initiate political action by agitation and propaganda—basically, yelling at everyone) became a common term; if you weren't a tub-thumping radical, you were a square.*

Feeling agitated.

Spurning traditional theater, small groups of amateurs set up shop in halls and clubs, including the "fringes" of the annual (and "high culture") Edinburgh festival. (Or were they just saving face because traditional theater spurned them?) Typical of such political groups was Portable Theater in Brighton, from which *David HARE* (b. 1947) and *Howard BRENTON* (b. 1942) emerged. They wrote *Brassneck* (1973) together, and many other works separately. Hare later moved to the establishment at the National. ("Grow up and sell out," as Lenny Bruce once said.)

*John McGRATH* (b. 1935) set up 7:84 Theater in 1971 (so called because 7 percent of the population then owned more than 80 percent of the wealth) as a company for his own plays, like *The Cheviot, The Stag,* and *The Black, Black Oil* (1973). McGrath tried to revive a socialist and popular theater, which working-class audiences saw in their own venues (village halls and so forth).

*David EDGAR* (b. 1948) wrote plays for the General Will company, targeting the Conservative government. He mainly wrote agitprop, but moved into socialist realism by the mid 1970s.

The first stage play of *Caryl CHURCHILL* (b. 1938), *Owners* (1972), was, like subsequent plays, motivated by her hatred of social injustice. *Light Shining in Buckinghamshire* (1976) and *Cloud Nine*

**Other Dreams**

Pretty much the only group from the 1960s in Britain still living the dream of popular theater created for local communities is Welfare State International. Founded in 1968 by John Fox, they create theater projects "to order," using carnival, processions, fireworks, dancing, and spectacular visual images in their shows.

**1969** BBC television's *Monty Python's Flying Circus* is a series of satirical, anarchic sketches, written and performed by a group of talented young actors.

**1972** Charlie Chaplin's *Limelight*, banned in the U.S. since 1952 because of the actor's alleged Communist sympathies, is finally rereleased.

**1979** Engineer Frank Rudy develops Nike's "Tailwind," the first air-cushioned trainer.

I wonder how many plays have scenes where men do this? (Churchill's *Cloud Nine*).

**PROMPT BOX**

A very influential figure of the time, though little remembered now, was Albert Hunt. After working with Peter Brook he went to Bradford College of Arts to teach, where he produced a restaging of the Russian Revolution in the streets with thousands of local residents (1967), and his own Brechtian play, *John Ford's Cuban Missile Crisis* (1970), with students of the college. They stopped short of executing the faculty, however.

In the U.S., *Ed BULLINS* (b. 1935) was inspired to write by Amiri Baraka's work. He has produced several highly successful plays, like *In the Wine Time* (1968) and *The Fabulous Miss Marie* (1971), which are as much influenced by jazz and blues music as any theater precedents. *Ntozake SHANGE* (b. 1948) is most famous for *For Colored Girls Who Have Considered Suicide When the Rainbow is Enuf* (1976), an interesting set piece of seven recitations of life experiences.

(1979) explored sexual role-playing, *Serious Money* (1987) savaged the sleazy activities of stockbrokers and traders (whether or not they quaked with fear is a well-kept secret). Unlike so many other "political" writers, Churchill has avoided pedantry, which gives her work an energy and theatrical variety.

Two colored girls considering their feet in Ntozake Shange's *For Colored Girls . . .*

**1963** A hotline is established between Washington and Moscow to try to prevent accidental wars.

**1974** Haile Selassie is deposed, ending the Solomonic Dynasty of Ethiopian emperors, which proverbially descends from Solomon and the Queen of Sheba.

**1976** 22 African nations boycott the Montreal Olympics, angered by the presence of New Zealand, which still has ties with South Africa.

1960~1990s

# Third World Voices

## Apartheid and Tyranny

*Since the 1970s, economic and social conditions in Third World countries have worsened, creating appalling levels of oppression, poverty, and dispossession. Independent of each other, many of the poor of these countries have turned to theater as a means of political expression. Theater is accessible to them, allowing perhaps the only voice available (until it gets crushed). The following are merely a tiny example of the vast range of work that has emerged from all over Africa, Asia, and the Americas.*

Wole Soyinka (1986) after receiving the Nobel Literature Prize.

Probably the most important playwright to come out of Africa has been the Nigerian *Wole SOYINKA* (b. 1934). His plays —for example, *A Dance of the Forests* (1960) and *A Play of Giants* (1984)—are complex, charting the difficulties faced by Yoruba cultural values in post-colonial Nigeria. In 1977, he produced a Nigerian version of Gay's *Beggar's Opera*, called *Opera Woyonsi*, which attacked Emperor Bokasa.

In South Africa, the white liberal writer *Athol FUGARD* (b. 1932) has claimed that his works, from *Boesman and Lena* (1969) through the "workshop" plays, including *Sizwe Banzi is Dead* (1972), are "regional," nonpolitical plays about individuals in specific situations.

**PROMPT BOX**

Augusto Boal wrote a book in 1983 called *The Theater of the Oppressed* (a subject he is well qualified to discuss). In it he refers to audiences as "spect-actors," which means they cocreate a play by offering different solutions to problems in the text. It's a good idea—we could have Lear tell his daughters to go jump in a lake, or Godot finally arrive!

**1982** King Sobhuza II of Swaziland dies at the age of 83, the world's longest-reigning monarch.

**1990** After 23 years of armed struggle, Namibia wins independence from South Africa and becomes an independent nation.

**1995** Nigerian writer and human rights activist Ken Saro-Wiwa is publicly executed as a political dissident.

### *Supporting Roles*

*Throughout South Africa in the 1970s, theater became the best means for blacks to reassert black nationalism, and their efforts influenced white liberals in existing theaters. Two of the most innovative companies were* **The Market Theater** *in Johannesburg and the* **Space Theater** *in Cape Town. Both provided venues for Fugard's plays.*

"We three kings." Athol Fugard and actors from *Sizwe Banzi*.

But they are clearly shaped by events from South Africa's political tensions. He has been attacked for not fully representing the black situation, but what he does very well is to interrogate a broader view of South African society as a whole, which is not only black. The success of *Sizwe Banzi* (based on the problems caused by the apartheid pass laws) and Fugard's "workshop" methods inspired director Barney Simon and his actors to cocreate *Woza Albert (1982)*, which toured the West to great acclaim.

In Brazil during the 1960s particular attention was paid to the success of North American groups like the Living Theater. American-trained *Augusto Boal* (b. 1931) began, in 1956, to produce Brecht-inspired political theater, such as *Revolution in South America* (1961), for the São Paulo Teatro Arena. After 1968, Brazil clamped down on such activities. Boal was tortured and imprisoned. In exile he continued his experiments into "teatro jornal" (documentary theater) and "teatro invisible" (public space theater), where spectators are unaware a rehearsed performance is happening.

**Oppressed Groups**

In Jamaica, a group of women have formed the company Sistren to articulate their plight as perhaps the most oppressed class of women in the Third World. They are now known internationally. The theater project of the Kenyan people of Kamiriithu, led by the playwright Ngugi wa Thiong'o, opposed the Kenyan dictatorship, only to have their plays banned, Thiong'o thrown into prison, and their theater bulldozed by the authorities.

**1950** The first sex change operation is performed in Denmark. New Yorker George Jorgensen becomes Christine.

**1957** Australian novelist, poet, and playwright Patrick White's novel *Voss* chronicles a Nietzschean German visionary's doomed expedition to cross the continent.

**1965** The Merchant-Ivory film *Shakespeare Wallah* follows a troupe of English actors touring India shortly after the end of British colonial rule.

1950~1990s

# Awakening Ex-Colonies

## Australia and Canada

*Black Australia has a dance-drama tradition traversing the (estimated) 40,000 years the aborigines have been there. Rituals relating to initiation, magic, and tribal ceremonies have been passed down from spiritual ancestors. In white Australia, however, attitudes toward the arts until the 1950s were largely divided into either urbanite sycophancy about all things English, or the antiart ignorance of the redneck.*

Aboriginal dance-dramas tell stories that relate the culture's social life and spiritual beliefs.

The American actor J. C. Williamson dominated Australian theater management for almost 60 years with imported English or American rubbish. "Australians don't want Australian" was his justification for not showing the slightest interest in either the country or its people. No one argued because he spiced the general pap he gave theatergoers with just enough "high culture" to keep the most obsequious (and influential) of them happy. This was why any local talent left just as soon as it could buy a ticket.

*The Summer of the Seventeenth Doll* (1955) by *Ray Lawler* (b. 1921) is probably still Australia's best-known play. It had an immediate and beneficial effect on playwriting, starting a "school" of three-act Realist plays. In the 1960s a copy of La Mama (see page 127) opened in Melbourne, producing a "café theater" company. In 1970 they moved to a local pram factory and changed their name to the Australian Performing Group. Their

**1980** In a vote on whether the predominantly French province of Québec should separate from Canada, 59.9 percent say no; in 1995 the percentage will be down to 51.

**1992** Queen Elizabeth II's "annus horribilis": two of her sons' marriages end in public scandal and fire breaks out at Windsor Castle. She will be the first British monarch to pay income tax.

**1997** Hong Kong becomes a "special administrative region" of China, in accordance with the terms of the 99-year lease agreed in 1898 between China and Britain.

excellent influence has been crucial in developing a very active and high-quality Australian "alternative" theater.

In Canada there exists a clear division between the English-speaking and French-speaking areas (quelle surprise!). As in Australia, early theater came from colonial masters, though the presence of a competitive French culture and a less isolating geographical position offset the worst effects of this. Companies like Manitoba Theater Centre (1958) began a regional movement, and Tarragon Theater (1970s) helped develop an alternative theater in the English language, but French Canadian culture has produced the most interesting physical, visual, and dramatic theater of the nation. Robert LePage, for example, stunned the world in the 1980s and 1990s with some of the most brilliantly visual theater ever seen in the West. He is exceptional for his interest in the experience of performance, and works like *The Seven Streams of the River Ola* are performed over several years, changing continually along the way.

**'Tit Coq**

The modern French Canadian theater began with the production, in 1948, of *'Tit Coq*, by Gratien Gélinas. Because the play was written in French and followed the search for identity of its protagonist, it seemed to speak for the whole of postwar French Canada. Its success was phenomenal, with over 500 performances in Québec (only the French could think a title like that was a good idea).

## *Supporting Roles*

*The Australian novelist* **Patrick White** *(1912–90) had four plays staged at university theaters in the 1960s. His use of Expressionist styles and almost caricatured characterization opened up new experimental avenues. The French Canadian writer* **Marcel Dubé** *(b. 1930) is the most influential Canadian playwright since 1950, with plays such as* Zone *(1955) and* Private Soldier *(1958).*

Robert LePage's *Elsinore* (1996) used slide projection and cinematic effects. He played Hamlet (and several other roles), but the star was the gigantic, ever-changing set.

**1964** International Tottenham Hotspur soccer player John White dies after being struck by lightning while sheltering under a tree.

**1968** British Conservative MP Enoch Powell attacks the British immigration policy: "As I look ahead I see the river foaming with much blood."

**1973** American film director, writer, and actor Woody Allen directs and stars in his futuristic comedy *Sleeper*.

1964 to the present

# Blurring the Boundaries

## Postmodernism

*"What is this thing called postmodernism?," I hear you cry. Well, it's a critic's term, which means real artists and people with blood in their veins ignore it. So should you. The phrase itself can describe only what it isn't, which is modernism, rather than clarify what it is. This vagueness sometimes makes it perfect for describing total garbage that no one understands, but will pay a lot for because they don't want to appear ignorant. Let's face it, art sometimes brings out the worst in people.*

Robert Wilson in *Hamlet*, 1996. His plays are visually interesting but tedious.

**Yawn . . .**

Typical of the Ontological-Hysteric Theater's productions was *Total Recall* (1970), where emotionless, untrained performers intoned monotonous dialogue while Foreman perched above them, sounding a buzzer every so often. This was done to "force [audiences] to another level of consciousness." Richard, dear heart, some of us can barely manage the lowest (like that in which you become aware that you're sitting in a theater, bored out of your mind).

What's more, all the so-called postmodern elements of pastiche, visible artifice, fiction seen as fiction, crossovers with other popular styles, etc., have existed in experimental theater since at least Alfred Jarry or the Dadaists.

*Robert Wilson* (b. 1941), American painter and director, constructs a visual theater. He has worked with brain-damaged children to create dreamlike pieces—for example, *A Letter to Queen Victoria* (1974) and *Einstein on the Beach* (1976)—where repetition and slow movement are deliberate. All his operalike pieces lack conventional plot, character, or "realistic" structures. The sense of time is altered, so crossing the stage can take an hour (watching it can seem like five!).

**Behind the Scenes**

After the first Robert Wilson production was shown in Europe (*Deafman Glance*, 1970), the Surrealist Louis Aragon wrote enthusiastically to his colleague André Breton, describing it as "what we from whom Surrealism was born dreamt would arise after us, beyond us . . ." So the tradition continues. But perhaps the letter was a Surrealist irony . . .

**1979** There are 21,456 murders reported in the U.S., more than half of which involved handguns.

**1986** Corazón Aquino is elected president of the Philippines, ousting Ferdinand Marcos; he and his shoe-buying wife, Imelda, have bled the country of an estimated $45 billion.

**1997** Mother Teresa, the Albanian-born nun who dedicated her life to caring for the poor of Calcutta, dies in the same week as Princess Diana.

Willem Dafoe was a regular in Wooster Group productions.

*Richard* FOREMAN (b. 1937) started his Ontological-Hysteric Theater in 1968. His intention, it seems, was to explore ontology (metaphysical science concerned with the state of "being"). The "hysteric" bit refers not to the name of the theater company, but to "classic middle-class, boulevard theater ... hysteric in its psychological topology" (oh well, that's all right, then).

*Arianne* MNOUCHKINE (b. 1934) creates collaborative pieces with her company, Théâtre du Soleil. Based on a mixture of Artaud and Brecht (now, that's living dangerously!), where both social problems and private angst could be examined, her creations include *The Clowns* (1969) and *Mephisto* (1979).

Arianne Mnouchkine's shows were invariably controversial.

Out of the Performance Group (see page 126) came the Wooster Group, under *Elizabeth* LECOMPTE (b. 1944). Works like *Rumstick Road* (1977) and *L.S.D.* (1984) were based on either the autobiographical splurges of company member Spalding Gray or the writings of Timothy Leary, with a bit of Miller's *The Crucible* thrown in (which Miller hated).

Théâtre du Soleil's Martine Frank: is she perhaps allergic to her makeup?

**1962** Rachel Carson publishes *Silent Spring*, warning of the dangers of pesticide use for wildlife.

**1972** Deranged Australian Laszlo Tuth attacks and damages Michelangelo's *Pietà* in Rome.

**1988** *Daedalus 88*, a man-powered aircraft, flies 74 miles over the Aegean.

1961 to the present

# Full Circle at Fin de Siècle?

## Theater Returns to Ritual and Dance

*As with all art after Modernism, what happens next? Sometimes it seems as if we've seen it, been there, done it, watched the video, and bought the T-shirt—or scrounged it at the press showing. But in a sense it's always been like that. Each new development has necessitated further new development. As the realities of life grow more complex, so does our need for, and methods of, expressing them.*

The actor as mannequin.

Theater in the West may well be dying in terms of "plays": the average age of audiences on Broadway is 45 and only about 7 percent of the population of Britain regularly sees theater at all, while movies and television thrive and interactive entertainments grow fast. Even in the East, traditional theaters like Nō are losing audiences to movies. But in the Third World, theater is still seen as a way of voicing political

**Mime**

Mime, which meant a form of comic folk play to the ancient Greeks and was then used to describe the performer, became a silent art in France during the 18th century, when dramatic monopoly stopped fairground "actors" from speaking. It has since developed through Jean-Louis Barrault, Marcel Marceau, and, in the U.S., Bread and Puppet Theater. 1960s intellectuals from Greenwich Village prized Marcel Marceau soundtrack albums as vital lifestyle props.

Jerome Savary's grand *Magic Circus* (1975), using traditional "types" from European theater.

concerns in ways the West has given up. Also, perhaps Western "live performance" can travel only in a nonrealistic direction now, as exemplified by Eugenio Barba, Jerome Savary, Peter Brook, Wilson, Foreman, and others of the avant-garde.

*Eugenio BARBA* (b. 1936) worked with Jerzy Grotowsky before founding the Odin Teatret, based in Holstebrö in Denmark. Odin is a center for theater research as well as a performing company, and a focus for the International School of Theater Anthropology. Barba has published his ideas in *The Floating Islands* (1984) and *Beyond "The Floating Islands"* (1986). In France, *Jerome SAVARY* (b. 1942) co-founded the Grand Théâtre Panique in the 1960s, which became the Grand Magic Circus after 1968. They produce highly successful, subversive part cabaret, part social satires, usually in nontheater spaces.

*Peter BROOK* (b. 1925) began at Birmingham Rep in the 1940s, moving on to the Royal Shakespeare Company 20 years later. Never content with traditional practices, he has moved ever onward and upward. Of course, as he became more imaginative and challenging, he had to leave Britain, so he moved to Paris, opening an International Center for Theater Research. His international company has performed productions including *The Conference of the Birds* (1976) and a nine-hour epic retelling of the entire Indian *Mahabharata* (1985)—and worth every one of the 32,400 seconds.

## Supporting Roles

**Tadeutz Kantor** *(b. 1915), the Polish director and painter, formed a group of artists called Cricot II in 1956. He has since produced happenings and theater pieces using actors as props and mannequins (and props and mannequins as actors?). He later developed the Theater of Death, with performances resembling seances.* **Pina Bausch** *explored sexual roles through mime and dance with her Wuppertal Tanztheater.*

# Glossary

*Get the vocab right! You don't wear an apron, live in a flat, or tidy your lawn with a rake.*

**ALIENATION EFFECT**
Any device used to help the audience perceive the stage "world" objectively as storytelling, thus stopping viewers from emotionally identifying with a character (e.g., visible stagehands or actors announcing who they are going to play).

**AMPHITHEATER**
An outdoor theater, like a half bowl with semicircular seating sloping down to the stage area; acoustics are excellent.

**ANGELS**
Financial backers of a production.

**APRON**
Part of a stage which projects out toward the audience.

**ARENA THEATER**
Originally, the oval Roman amphitheater where audience surrounded the stage area.

**BEGINNERS**
1) Those actors who appear first on stage.
2) A call given by stage managers to get them there (five minutes before curtain).

**BOX SET**
A set of three sides—mainly used to imitate a room (the audience looks through an imaginary "fourth wall").

**BUSINESS**
Activities invented by "realist" actors to reinforce character (e.g., nervously fiddling with things), or to make them appear as if they have a purpose for being there.

**CORPSE**
Uncontrollable giggling by actors on stage (used as a verb—to corpse): caused by a) drunkenness, b) nervousness, c) forgetfulness, d) the sudden realization that the play is dreadful.

**CUE-TO-CUE**
Technical rehearsal to allow the crew to work through all the cues (lighting, scene changes, etc.).

**CYCLORAMA**
A plain screen extending around the performing space for image projection or simply to give a feeling of infinite space.

**DARK**
A term used to describe a theater closed to the public, even temporarily.

**DEUS EX MACHINA**
An event or person who "appears" in the nick of time to save a situation (originally Greek—"a god from a machine," where gods were suspended above the stage ready to descend).

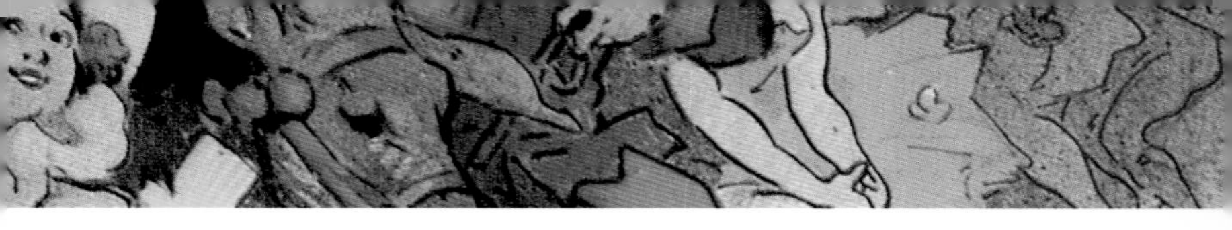

**DIORAMA**
A three-dimensional illusion created by painted cloth and cleverly focused lights.

**DOWNSTAGE**
Part of stage closest to the audience.

**DRESS REHEARSAL**
The final rehearsal before opening, originally intended to ensure that all costumes were finished. It is also, as Alfred Jarry noted: "… a free show for a select group of artists and friends of the author, and where for one unique evening the audience is almost expurgated of idiots."

**FLAT**
An element of scenery made of a wooden frame covered in painted canvas or plywood.

**FOOTLIGHTS**
A batten of lights on the edge of the stage. First used around 1670, but no longer necessary.

**FOURTH WALL**
An imaginary wall between audience and players.

**GREEN ROOM**
A room near the stage for actors to rest and exchange gossip.

**PRINCIPALS**
The lead actors in a play.

**PROSCENIUM ARCH**
An archway, or division, between auditorium and stage.

**RAKE**
An area of stage sloping down to the audience to improve sightlines.

**ROSTRUM**
A piece of portable staging. Usually a box-like platform, which might link to other rostra to raise parts of the action.

**RUN-THROUGH**
A rehearsal where all the bits of a production are put in the right order. Better known as a "stagger through."

**STAGE LEFT**
Left-hand side from the cast's view. Stage right is the opposite.

**SUBTEXT**
A set of meanings lurking beneath the "surface" meaning of a play that are usually and mysteriously known only to the director.

**THEATER IN THE ROUND**
Any auditorium where the audience sits around a central stage.

**THRUST STAGE**
Staging that projects into the audience so they sit on either side.

**UPSTAGE**
The part of the stage farthest from the audience, or—as a verb—the time-honored practice of scene-stealing.

**WINGS**
Areas at the side of the stage hidden from the audience's view.

# Old Thespian Sayings and Superstitions

*Actors are under a lot of pressure, darling, with all those beastly lines to learn, costumes that aren't always as flattering as they should be, and directors that make Hitler seem like Mother Teresa. They have their own little ways of coping.*

**BREAK A LEG**
Traditionally a good-luck greeting between thespians.

**FALL DOWN BACKWARD**
Another thespian good-luck greeting.

**FIRE**
Unlucky word in theater generally. This is from the time when candles and gas were used and often sent the building up in flames. Hence "fireproofing" is the First Commandment for technicians.

**FRIBBLE**
A word used to describe the ad-libbing actors did when they forgot lines in the 17th century. These days it's simply known as "drivel."

**MACBETH**
Unlucky to speak this name or quote from the play in a theater. The play has been dogged by bad luck since the boy actor playing Lady Macbeth died as it opened in 1606. It is always referred to as "The Scottish Play" instead.

**ONION AT THE END**
A music-hall term meaning any action/lines at the end of a play designed to get the audience crying.

**SKIN OFF YOUR NOSE**
19th-century thespian good-luck greeting. Coarse makeup would literally peel skin from an actor's face after a performance; so "Skin off your nose" meant "Hope you stay in work!"

**SPIT AND DRIBBLE**
The cheapest seats in the house, usually on the highest balcony from where wags would spit and dribble on wealthier theatergoers below.

**THE OLD COMPLAINT**
A thespian euphemism for drunkenness.

**WHISTLING**
It was considered bad luck to whistle while in the Green Room. If you do, you must turn around three times, leave the room for one minute, knock three times, and reenter! Not a good idea if you're suffering from "the old complaint."

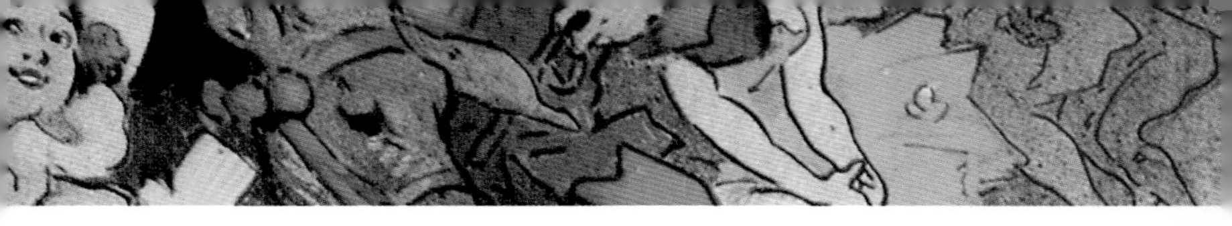

# Notable Performances

*Some shows quietly close after a few weeks or transfer swiftly to the sticks. A few go down in the annals (yes, I said ann-a-l-s) of time and create theater history—although not always for the right reasons.*

#### BREAKING NEW GROUND

Don't you wish you'd seen Stanislavsky's first collaboration with Chekhov—*The Seagull* at the Moscow Art Theater, 1896? Or the première of Beckett's *Waiting for Godot* in Paris in 1953? Or the day snoozing British theater woke up to John Osborne's *Look Back in Anger* in 1956?

#### GENDER ISSUES

When Margaret Hughes played Desdemona in 1660, she was the first professional actress in British theater.

#### "I DIED OUT THERE, DARLING!"

In *Le Mystère du Nouveau Testament* at Valenciennes, 1547, the actor playing the Devil was gutted and hanged by mistake.

The author and lead actor Molière died on stage during a production of *The Imaginary Invalid*, Comédie Française, Paris, 1673.

On April 14, 1865, President Lincoln was shot by an actor, John Wilkes Booth, while watching *Our American Cousin* at Ford's Theater in Washington.

#### TECHNICAL HITCHES

The first production ever of *Henry VIII*, June 29, 1613, resulted in the Globe Theater burning to the ground (see page 35).

The 1912 *Hamlet* at the Moscow Arts Theater was memorable because Craig's gigantic set collapsed.

*Hair*, London 1966, marked the first time a penis had been seen on the British stage.

#### WHAT A RIOT!

Plays that have inspired the audience to riot include Jarry's *Ubu Roi*, Paris, 1896, and Synge's *Playboy of the Western World*, New York, 1911.

#### WHEN'S INTERMISSION?

Peter Brook's *Mahabharata*, Avignon, 1985, lasted for nine hours.

Ken Campbell directed *The Warp*, Edinburgh, Scotland, 1979, lasting 24 hours.

John Arden's *The Non-Stop Connolly Show* (1975) took 26½ hours to perform in the Irish Republic's capital, Dublin.

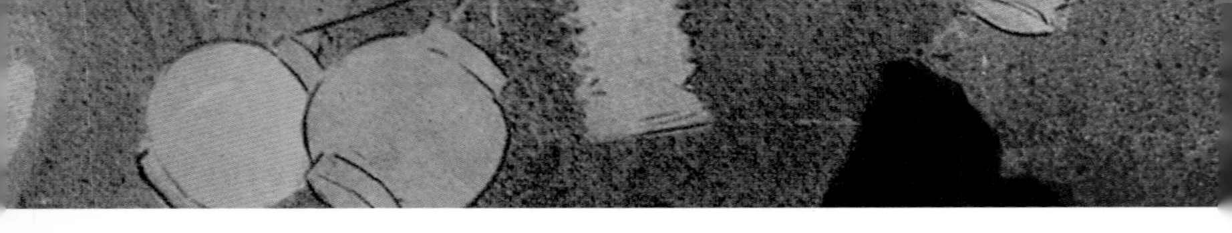

# Index

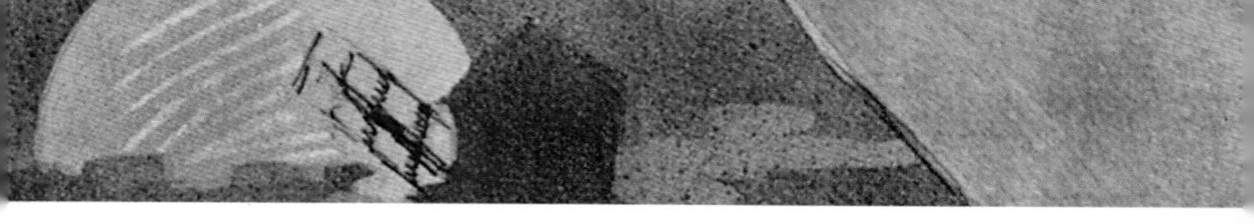

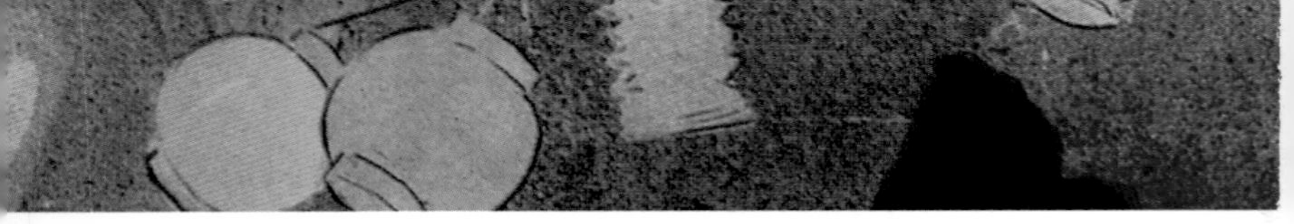

## PHOTOGRAPHIC CREDITS

**Archiv für Kunst und Geschichte, London:** 18, 19, 22, 23 (Staatliche Kunstsammlungen Kassel), 25 (Palazzo Vecchio, Florence), 29 (SMPK Nationalgalerie, Berlin), 30 (Sherborne Castle, Dorset), 39 (Schloss Augustusburg Bruhl), 64 (Goethe Gallerie), 65 (Gemälde von Anton Graff), 76, 78, 94, 95B, 96, 102 (Hugh Lane Municipal Gallery), 107 (Bühnen Archiv Oskar Schlemmer), 124T, 134.

**AKG, London/Herbert Kraft:** 12/13B.

**AKG, London/Eric Lessing:** 13, 26, 27. (Louvre, Paris), 60 (Château Ferney-Voltaire).

**AKG, London/Jean Louis-Nou:** 53 (Asiatic Society of Bombay).

**The Bridgeman Art Library:** 24 (Villa Farnesina, Rome), 28 (Phillips Fine Art), 32 (Corpus Christi College, Cambridge), 43 (Victoria and Albert Museum), 48 (Phillips Fine Art), 55 (British Museum), 56 (Stapleton College), 62 (Casa Goldoni, Venice), 63T (Galleria degli Uffizi), 70 (Museum of the City of New York), 83 (Nasjonal Galleriet, Oslo), 106 (Phillips Fine Art).

**BAL/Roger Viollet:** 40 (Musée du Breuil de St.-Germain, Langres).

**Corbis, London:** 98 (Robbie Jack), 89 (Austrian Archive).

**Corbis-Bettman:** 80, 99, 115T, 129 (UPI).

**e. t. archive, London:** 17, 35, 44, 46, 50, 66, 68, 72, 73.

**Hulton Getty, London:** 92, 93, 110T (H. Guttman), 110B, 118, 119, 120 (Polkington), 122, 131, 136 (Fred Mott).

**Magnum/Martine Franck:** 135B, 135R.

**Performing Arts Library, London:** 33, 61, 76T.

**PAL/Clive Barda:** 63B.

**PAL/Henrietta Butler:** 103.

**PAL/Ben Christopher:** 109, 111, 128.

**PAL/Fritz Curzon:** 117.

**PAL/Ivan Kinci:** 43R.

**PAL/Michael Ward:** 97.

**PAL/John Wender:** 54.

**Rex Features:** 114, 119, 123T, 123B, 124B, 130, 132, 135T.

**The Stock Market, London:** 57, 58, 85.

**Emmanuel Valette/courtesy of Cultural Industries:** 133.

**Reg Wilson, London:** Title page, 11, 36, 37, 41, 49, 59, 82, 85, 90, 95T, 112, 121, 125, 126, 127.

## COPYRIGHT